BROKEN HEART
WHOLE HEART

A Family and Addiction

BROKEN HEART
WHOLE HEART
A Family and Addiction

Pecki Sherman
and
Virginia Newlin

Hampshire Books
Akron ● Philadelphia
1989

Cover design: Richard Kish

Library of Congress Cataloging-in-Publication Data

Sherman, Pecki 1939-
  Broken heart whole heart: a family and addiction / Pecki Sherman and Virginia Newlin
      p.   cm.
  ISBN 1-877674-01-X
  1. Sherman, Josh. 2. Narcotic addicts—United States—Biography. 3. Sherman, Pecki, 1939-   . 4. Mothers—United States—Biography. 5. Mothers and sons—United States—Case studies. 6. Narcotic addicts—United States—Family relationships—Case studies. 7. Narcotic addicts—Rehabilitation—United States—Case studies.
  I. Newlin, Virginia, 1920-   . II. Title.
  HV5805.S53S47 1989
  362.29´13´0922—dc20
  [B]   89-11167

Printed in the United States of America

Dedicated to:

Sixer, Sunshine and Tenzing
Dubie, Sara and William

Contents

Preface

This book is a story of two stories, both Pecki's, neither one of which can stand alone. One story is about her fight for health and connectedness with the joy and mystery of the universe. The other story is about her son, Josh, and the drug addiction that was destroying him — destroying the whole family, in fact — and how help came to them in time. The stories become one story of the triumph of spirit.

"There's nothing as whole as a broken heart."

attributed to Reb Nahman of Bratzlav
a Hasidic Master (1772-1810)

Chapter 1

Green Tomato Soup

Sixer, our German Shepherd mix, was playing catch-you with Tenzing, the tiger cat, Sixer's tongue lolling out, his brown eyes fixed on the cat's fluffy tail as it threaded swiftly through an azalea bush. Dubie, our Hungarian sheep dog — looking, as usual, like a tangled ball of black yarn — skidded through yellow ginkgo leaves at Sixer's heels.

In a way, Tenzing kept us together, I said to myself. At least he gave us something non-controversial that we could talk about. I was right to name him Tenzing, for the conqueror of Everest. Without Tenzing, Hillary never would have made it. And we might not have either.

Without Tenzing, Paul and I might be divorced. Without Tenzing, I and/or Josh could be dead. Without Tenzing, I would not be sitting in the early autumn sun quartering tomatoes for green tomato soup.

It was late fall in 1982. An abundance of green tomatoes in the garden and an impending frost was my excuse for a small dinner party. Indian summer was already over, and the promised frost would blanch the pink impatiens, blacken the tomatoes, and turn their solid flesh to water. Bright and cold, tonight's stars would be dancing as the garden died. I had already canned sixty jars of sauce: tomatoes with squash, basil, peppers, onions — whatever the garden produced — and today there were hundreds of green tomatoes staring at me accusingly. I gathered as many as I could, and, comfortable in a wool sweater in the afternoon sun, quartered them while my dogs and cats played in the leaves.

Carrying the large bowl into the kitchen, I breathed in the faint smell of burning wood from the wood stove, a smell that hinted at tranquility and well-being and affection. The farmhouse dining room, beamed, plastered and 18th century, was already blazing with zinnias, nasturtiums and marigolds placed in small containers on tables, on deep window sills, and on the mantelpiece of the cook-in fireplace.

The evening's guests were to be old friends, and, as it happened, the men invited were professionals in the medical field.

The menu was to be green tomato soup served with a bubbling Gruyere cheese topping and hard-crusted bread, followed by baked flounder, stir-fried gingered broccoli and the last green salad from the garden. Dessert would be deep-dish apple pie and ice cream.

At the dinner table that evening, the talk began with the computer-based hospital systems company, of which Paul was vice-president.

"I see the stock has gone up again," said the GP. "I bought my wife a hundred shares, and she's already made a profit, haven't you, dear?"

"How's your tennis game, Paul?" asked the gynecologist.

"I played this morning, 6-2, 6-love." He smiled, his blue eyes twinkling behind silver-rimmed glasses, but I knew the truth. Paul was the love.

"How's your back, Porter?" Paul asked the gynecologist.

"Still bothering me some; I'm swimming, though, and that helps."

"How about acupuncture?" I asked eagerly. "That's supposed to help back problems. It opens the blockage, you know, and the energy flow becomes smoother. It would work perfectly with your swimming."

"There she goes again," said the dentist. "Our resident health expert."

Everybody laughed, and I, embarrassed and a little hurt,

looked from the bright flowers in their bowls to the door leading to the terrace and outside. Outside, the silence was crisp and cool. Outside was a harvest moon and a friendly tree, lots of friendly trees.

"Never mind. We still love you, Pecki . . . What's with you, Bob?" the dentist said, turning to the psychiatrist on his right.

"Worked to death," said the psychiatrist. "Don't even have time for my oriental rug collection. By the way, that's a beautiful Sarouk upstairs in your guest room, Paul."

"Actually, that's Pecki's dog's bedroom. He sleeps in the brass bed, you know."

"Well, as long as he doesn't pee on that rug. You ought to bring it downstairs, Paul."

The talk drifted into hospital-patient stories, and I thought about Josh, our sixteen-and-a-half year old son, a recovering drug addict. Josh was definitely patient material, but none of these doctors would have been able to help him. It took alternate methods to help Josh. His recovery involved taking him off drugs and alcohol. I thought of the many doctors and counselors we had seen — not one of them had identified drugs as the cause of the problem — of the many experts who stopped with the diagnosis that Josh was a difficult child. "Over-anxious disorder of adolescence," said the psychiatrist and his bill for one-and-a-half months of treatment was $3790.00. We were lucky our insurance could cover it.

"How's Josh, Pecki?" asked the GP, as if he'd caught my brain waves.

"Oh, he's doing marvelously and he's back in school. He's been drug-free for five months." I wondered to myself whether Josh would like the Catholic Brothers in his new school. "A Jewish kid in a Catholic school," I said out loud, "but it's a caring environment, and since he's living out of state, we would have to pay school tuition anyway."

I thought about the program Josh was in and last month's open meeting when Josh had run across the room—his face radiant—and hugged me and cried. We both had cried. "I love you, Mom," he'd said. "I love you, Josh. I love you!"

I looked around the dinner table and smiled at my friends.

"We have a delicious home-made apple pie for dessert—not mine, unfortunately. Who wants ice cream with it? And how about coffee or tea?"

I got up to fill the orders.

Into the kitchen drifted scraps of conversation.

"There's this new drug on the market . . ."

Oh, my God, I thought, another new drug to cover up symptoms, and they never see beyond them to the cause. I concentrated on serving the apple pie, feeling myself withdrawing from them, those good doctors who, I knew, had saved many lives, those caring friends, who chose their ignorance. They were not interested that I no longer needed medication for constant sinus problems, allergies, earaches and headaches—chronic conditions that had been treated for 20 years with antihistamines and antibiotics. Not interested that I no longer needed medication to bring on my menstrual cycle and to fight pre-menstrual symptoms. Using alternate methods of cure, I had been medication free for the past year-and-a-half. I had stopped the pill popping advocated by the media and encouraged by easy prescriptions from some of the medical profession, and, as I relied less on drugs and more on nontraditional health methods such as dream interpretation and acupuncture, I gained physical and emotional strength. I was no longer a pushover for everything my husband and children demanded of me, no longer the scapegoat who accepted the guilt for whatever went wrong.

For over four years—ever since Josh was twelve—I had been going through misery and guilt over his problems: his increasingly secretive behavior, his failures in school, and his ugliness to me and his younger brother Jonathan. I thought that they must be my fault, must be the result of things I had done or neglected to do in raising him. After all, he was an adopted child and should have received especially devoted care. Perhaps I had not shown my devotion enough. Perhaps he thought I loved Jonathan, my birth child, better. Possibly his lack of interest in sports was because I hadn't allowed him to get up at 5 a.m. to play ice hockey before school when he was eight years old. I told him, No, he needed his rest. Since I would have had to get up too in order to drive him to the hockey rink, that also applied to me, but maybe, if I'd made that sacrifice, he wouldn't have faked illness in order to avoid sports when he was older.

That was the kind of reproach I dished out to myself. Until the past summer of 1982 I was convinced that whatever I had done with Josh had been wrong and that I was responsible for the family's disasters. But I didn't know how or why. Until my health improved, I was not able to think clearly or deal with the increasing problems. While improved health didn't keep me or my family from spiraling into crisis, it did work for our survival. I became able to think clearly again, make progress at one level or another, even during dark, obsessive, painful times.

Like the time last spring when Paul's cousin Sara, a zoologist, was visiting when Josh strode in the front door, a bare knife stuck into a chain around his leg, a dirty bandanna on his head, and an ugly loose bicycle chain swinging in his hand; dirty looking, grungy all over, his eyes, as usual, scowling hate at me. Mommy-bitch, Mommy-whore, who always stood in his way.

Ever since two years before when I had sent him to juvenile detention for stealing Paul's Fiat, Josh had hated me. I hated myself too after we had him released and found out that his arm had been broken. But I had felt that some action had to be taken. Josh was only 14 and was out of control. He had stolen the car twice, was, I felt sure, likely to steal it again. Paul was away on a business trip, so when the police asked me, "What do you want us to do with him, Mrs. Sherman?" I said, "Take him away." It was overreaction on my part to constant provocation on his. He was manipulative, continually breaking family rules. I hoped it would teach him a lesson, and I was too angry to think what other consequences there might be. Later on, I panicked. I tried to get in touch with him at the detention center but couldn't.

When Paul and I went to the courthouse to bring him home, we saw the broken arm. "I broke it playing basketball," Josh said defiantly.

"Oh, that was hard luck!" I should have felt sorrier than I did. "Tell us about the center, Josh."

"The meals were better than yours, anyway."

That brat! I stopped feeling sorry for him at all — and he was already hating me. Hating me, as two years later he was doing in his bicycle chains and dirty bandanna.

Where the hell did he get those clothes and where the hell did he change into them this time? I asked myself. Every school morning he goes out with his jacket and tie, comes home without them, and I never see that jacket go up to his room.

And then I stopped wondering about that problem and was frightened, thoroughly frightened, by my light-haired, dimpled, six-foot-tall, sixteen-year-old son, who was standing in the doorway staring at me with hooded eyes, saying nothing, but following me with his hate as I turned my back and left the hallway, trying my best to walk casually, keep my shoulders straight, even though I felt that knife might strike me between my shoulder blades.

It was no exaggeration. Over and over, Josh threatened to get rid of me any way he could. One way, he suggested, was to siphon the brake fluid out of my car so that when I put my foot on the brake, nothing would happen. The car would crash, I would die, and he would be free. Never again would I be able to cause him problems, check up on him, call his friends' parents, call the school.

"I'm going to get rid of you, asshole. You're going to leave here, and Dad and I will be alone. Then we'll be happy," he would whisper to me over and over, whisper so that nobody else could hear.

Now, I heard him follow me to the kitchen. Sara was in the guest bedroom, lying on Sixer's bed after a long day's research at the zoo. There was nobody else in the house. Nobody to help me against Josh.

He cornered me at the sink.

"I'm going out now, whore, and you can't stop me." He swung his chain.

"You'll do nothing of the kind. You're going to do your homework and then you can ask permission to go out." Would he strike me with that chain? My flesh shrank with the certainty of it.

"Bitch, I'll do what I want to do! You can't stop me!"

Not with a knife in the chest, I thought. We were standing rigidly, my nose to his chest, my fists clenched, my eyes on the knife, while I wondered if I could knee him in the groin if I had to. He was tall, solid, powerful, in spite of the drugs. He could hurt me easily, kill me if he wanted to, as, more and more often, I wanted to kill him. I reached behind me into the sink of dirty dishes, fumbling for a kitchen knife.

At this point, Sara came bopping into the room. I saw her start and stare at Josh's back, taking a good look at the chains, knife, and bandanna.

"Could I have a cup of tea, please, Pecki?" she asked, her voice sounding as ordinary as if there wasn't a Hell's Angel standing in the bright farmhouse kitchen. "How about you, Josh?"

He gave a shake of his head and turned towards Sara, showing his dimple in a little-boy smile that was heart-breaking to me.

"Well then, come into the living room and talk to me for a while," suggested Sara.

To my astonishment, he went, and later, to my even greater astonishment, he appeared without the knife, chain and bandanna, and with Sara, who requested that he be allowed to go out with his friends until ten.

"It's very important to the child," she said. I nodded,

very glad that somehow Sara had diffused the situation. Josh had won perhaps, but nobody had been hurt.

When Paul came home, to be greeted by the dogs at the door, I told him about Josh and the chains. Paul just looked tired, his blue eyes dull. "Oh, you're exaggerating, Pecki."

"Exaggerating! Never in my wildest dreams could I have conjured up that costume."

"Well then, how long was that knife anyway? What color was the bandanna? How did he fasten the chain around his leg? With a bicycle lock? Was it a bicycle chain or what?"

"Oh, go to hell, Paul! What you're saying is that I made it up, you bastard!" Let them live together, they deserve each other, I thought.

And again in came Sara. "Ask Sara, if you don't believe me. She saw him. In fact, she talked him out of his weapons."

"That's right. You've got a problem, Paul," said Sara. She'd changed her clothes and had on a soft mauve sweater and a pair of slacks. Her dark hair was brushed, her face made up, but in the center of her forehead there were two new vertical lines.

"I'm going upstairs to change," said Paul, leaving the room.

Sara and I looked at each other and shook our heads.

"He's driving me crazy, or maybe I am crazy. At least *he* thinks so. He thinks there's nothing wrong with Josh or else I'm causing it. Help me, Sara."

Later, at dinner in the kitchen around the maple table, a small fire in the wood-burning stove to cut the chill of the April evening and daffodils in an earthenware crock, Sara started talking about Josh's behavior.

"Hostile," she said.

"How is your mother, Sara?" asked Paul.

"Oh, for God's sake, Paul, don't change the subject again," I interjected. "Don't you see you're forcing us to live a lie?"

Paul carefully buttered a slice of bread, broke it into quarter-size pieces and popped one into his mouth, chewing on it in a concentrated manner.

Sara bounced from her seat, ran around the table, shook Paul by his shoulders, and burst into tears.

"This is the worst day I've spent in my life. Your son is totally out of control. Obviously he's on drugs or something. He's threatening his mother. He'll kill her or she'll kill him, and you sit there chewing your bread. What's the matter with you, Paul? Don't you care if your family self-destructs? And I always so admired you. I must have been crazy."

"Well, maybe you are, Sara. You certainly are overreacting."

Sit quietly and let Sara get his attention, I told myself, running my fingers around the dinner plate's yellow rim. I wiped my finger on the napkin and ran it around the plate again. If I should divorce Paul, what will happen to Jonathan? My finger continued around the rim and I choked on a silent scream. What will happen to Jonathan?

"Overreacting?" shrieked Sara. "The truth is I can't react as strong as the situation deserves."

"Strongly," corrected Paul.

"But Paul, don't you see what's happening?"

"Yes, I see, but I don't know what to do about it!"

Chapter 2

Grandmothers

Neither of us had known what to do about Josh, but, at least, I had been looking for help ever since his rebellion had gone beyond normal adolescence.

I was prepared for slacking off on school work and a certain amount of sneaking off to smoke cigarettes behind the barn. Missing the school bus by oversleeping was customary kid behavior, but Josh went far beyond that. There were mornings when it was literally impossible to wake him. I would call to him, go into his room, shake him, yell in his ear, but there would be no response. On other mornings, he would be up early, bright and cheerful, and I would think that I must have been imagining the times when everything about him seemed wrong.

My moods were dependent on his behavior. When he was cheerful, I was too. I could have seen the problem if he had been someone else's child, but it was only gradually that I realized that what was going on in my family was very bad indeed. Something had to be done.

I began by consulting the usual sources of help: doctors and school counselors. Nothing they suggested worked, and, by the spring of 1982, the behavior of my sixteen-year-old son was even more rude and ugly and frightening. He was failing in school, persecuting his younger brother, disobeying his father and terrifying me.

If Paul noticed my terror, he did nothing to alleviate it. In fact, he acted as if the problems with Josh were all mine. No matter what awful thing I told him had happened, Paul looked unruffled. "If you'll just ignore it, Pecki, the problem will go away." What was going away, it seemed to me, was my good marriage, the husband who had loved and trusted me as I did him. Our love, our family life, Josh's character, my stability, and my health were all going.

For many years I had had small health problems: headaches, earaches, sinus infections, poor circulation, and menstrual disorders. Medical help temporarily improved but never eliminated them, and now they seemed to be getting worse. Everything was getting worse. Everything had turned sour and bitter. It seemed long and far away, like sunlight across a far field, when our family life had been happy.

I remembered one particular morning in Marquand Park when Josh had been seven and Jonathan four-and-a-half and Paul had taken them to look for the chocolates he had hidden ahead of time in the low branches of spreading Japanese maples, dogwoods, and flowering cherry trees.

"These choc'lats are sure hard to find this time, Dad."

"It was your elves that hid them, wasn't it, Dad?"

"From your choc'lat factory in Scotland," said Jonathan, as he scrambled into an apple tree which had dropped its blossoms.

"Those elves knocked all the flowers off this tree, Dad." Josh scuffed his sneakers through thick white petals.

"That's right, Josh. I hope the park guards didn't catch them."

"Maybe you'd better call Scotland and see," said Jonathan around a mouthful of Hershey Buds.

They're all enjoying the game, I thought, and the boys never question their father's fictional chocolate factory. It was a joyful sight: my three men treasure hunting, finding the best treasure of all, a mutual love and trust. Paul was the boys' Danny Kaye, their smiling story teller who brought magic into their lives, who was always able to make a child feel special.

And certainly our sons were special. Jonathan—brown hair, sparkling brown eyes, a constant smile, slender; already at four-and-a-half, a trapeze artist on tree branches. And Josh—a handsome little boy, blond hair, brown eyes, pink cheeks—solid, a fine athlete, playing Midget Little League baseball and soccer—highly inquisitive, turning over stones to see who's living there, spending hours sifting water through his fingers to look for life, a child both shy and aggressive at the same time. With his peers, Josh was a leader and innovator. He put new twists in old games and organized the players, barking orders like a drill sergeant. But in front of adults, he was quiet and shy. "What a polite little boy Josh is," the adults would say.

When he was little he would pick flowers (from the neighbors' gardens, often as not) and hand them to me with a loving expression in his soft brown eyes. But later on, from the time he was fourteen, he'd just as soon bring them to my grave, I thought. And maybe he would have too, if a variety of ways to get help hadn't found me.

I had started going to ToughLove meetings after hearing a radio program about misbehaving teenagers and parents who had lost control. That's us, I'd thought, and sent for their booklet. It came with a question-and-answer sheet.

Is your child missing days at school?

Grades dropping? Friends changing?

Is your child secretive? Disrespectful?

Yes, I said. Yes. Yes. Yes. And yes, they said, meant that the child was displaying a pattern of drug abuse.

At fourteen, Josh was breaking curfew, not getting up in the morning for school, turning ugly and mean. He was beginning to look like a hood.

The ToughLove meetings gave me a chance to be honest about what was happening, to tell the truth about my child's behavior and to get support from other people. Paul saw no problem, and, of course, wouldn't go.

Another source of support had come to me three years earlier as the result of a conversation at a dinner party with four old friends.

The Popkins had just come back from a vacation, but, instead of telling us about their supposed trip to California, they told us about a week-long self-help program they had attended in Virginia.

"We practiced achieving states of higher consciousness," said Phyllis.

"Higher consciousness?" asked Helen in a shall-I-believe-what-I'm hearing tone of voice.

"Where you become aware of other levels of under-standing. We got psychic messages," said eye surgeon, Arnie Popkin.

"And we're moving to Charlottesville, " said Phyllis, who was on the board of the League of Women Voters.

"But what about your practice, Arnie?" asked Paul, twiddling the salt shaker.

"I'm going into general practice, applying to lecture at the University of Virginia, too. I've been wanting to get out of surgery for quite a while, Paul."

"Leave Princeton? Leave that marvelous practice? Two offices, other doctors working under you, throw it all over?"

The Popkins looked at each other and smiled, "We've already bought a house in Charlottesville. Arnie saw it in a dream," said Phyllis, "and we found it."

My God, I thought, as I pulled at my hair which was curling tighter from the conversation. They're under a spell. They've been caught by the world's greatest charlatan.

"What about your children?" asked Helen.

"The girls are due to change schools next year anyway. Linda will be able to keep her horse down the road, and our little one is excited about joining the soccer team."

For several days, I mulled over the conversation. The Popkins had been involved in unorthodox things before: Yoga, Transcendental Meditation, Bio-feedback, inner voices, psychics, and even knew people who went "out of body." But to give up Arnie's career, their community posi-tions? I decided that I had to do something for them: find out the truth; at least, check out one of their charlatans, some-body local, the psychic Jean Hastings Quinn, to whom the Popkins went for readings. I would prove that Quinn was a fake, and, therefore, that the path they were following (which for an unknown reason was threatening to me) was ridiculous. I asked Helen to go with me to see Jean Quinn.

During breakfast of the morning of the appointment, I complained to Paul. "I know I just gave up my part-time job to be a full-time mother, but I can't stand all this driving. Every afternoon I have to take somebody somewhere and often at the same time. You're never around to help me. If you're not working, you're playing tennis. We never have dinner together, and you don't see the boys except on week-ends. And my allergies have started to bother me again."

"I'll rearrange my schedule so I can be home for dinner more," said Paul.

"That will be nice." I kissed him gratefully.

For him that was quite a concession.

A few minutes later, Helen's car pulled into our driveway and we set off for Jean Quinn's. It was a beautiful spring day, a beautiful drive over the countryside to Jean Quinn's house. We were a little surprised at the ordinariness of it when we got there. It was a simple, neat, attractive, suburban house, gray stone, blue shutters, and Jean Quinn herself bore no trappings of mysticism. A bright pleasant-looking woman, she had a straightforward manner. I was the first to have a reading. I went into her office, sat down at one side of a round polished wood table. Jean Quinn asked my name and birth date. Then she lowered her head, cupped her eyes with her fingers and said:

"You're sorry you gave up your job. You can't stand all the driving you have to do. Your husband is never around to help you. He doesn't see the children, except on weekends. You're feeling frustrated and alone." She went on talking, telling me things about myself that resonated as truth, while I sat on my side of the table in almost a state of shock.

Suddenly, I felt a surge of electricity through my body. A

coursing of electricity, chills and goosebumps, as though I had been plugged into an outlet. I felt around under the table as sneakily as I could, sure that it was wired, but I could feel nothing with my fingertips. I shifted my chair so I could reach farther underneath, but still touched nothing, and the tingling in my body continued. Finally, it was too much. "I'm feeling a lot of electricity," I said.

"There's someone here who wants to see you — who says that . . . that it isn't your fault. Perhaps this person is a grandmother. Think about a grandmother."

At once I thought of my father's mother, my wonderful Bubba, who always smelled like fresh-baked bread. When I was a small child, she lived with us in a row house above the fruit and vegetable store she and my Zayda owned in South Philadelphia. "It's Bubba," I said, and as soon as I mentioned Bubba's name, the electric feeling went away, even though the remark about it *not being my fault* made no sense.

I didn't know what it could have meant, but I dismissed the remark and was able to share in the conversation as Jean accurately described my life, husband, children, and health problems. Jean had a soft comforting manner, and I began to like her quite a bit. Her red hair and her manner reminded me of my first-grade teacher.

Again, the electricity started surging through my body. This time it was accompanied by a pounding in my head, not a headache, but a pounding so loud that I thought Jean must surely hear it. At the same time, something told me that Bubba was the wrong person.

"The electricity is back, and I think that we've been talking about the wrong person. I don't think it's Bubba."

"Well, let me describe her to you," said Jean. She straightened her back and neck, slowly raised her hands to her forehead and drew them behind her head, pulling her hair into a bun. She said, "She's rather aristocratic ... firm ... remote ... determined." Jean's face reflected a stern look. She took on the mannerisms of my Grandmother Zorn.

"It's . . . not . . . your . . . fault," Jean said slowly.

As I heard the words, I heaved a deep sigh and the electricity left my body. I felt a lightness, as if an actual weight had been lifted from my shoulders, a weight I had been carrying since I was twelve and Grandmother Zorn had hung herself in our basement.

Grandmother Zorn was born in Russia into a wealthy Jewish family of doctors, lawyers, and judges. In the early 1900s, this beautiful young woman came alone to America to marry her cousin. In 1908, their first child, my mother, was born.

By 1917, the time of the Russian Revolution, Grandmother Zorn had learned that her family had lost land, wealth, position. Eventually they also lost their lives. She never got over the shock. She lost interest in everything except her garden, where she talked to each flower as if it were a friend. She was able to show her plants the love that she could not show her daughter or grandchildren. After destroying the few old addresses and letters she had from her family in Russia—thus severing all connections—she hung herself in our basement while baby-sitting for us one evening.

"I've never been conscious of blaming myself for her death," I said as I finished the story. "But I never went into a dark basement again."

Somehow I had taken on the weight of my grandmother's death, just as my mother and father had taken on Holocaust refugees. During my childhood, my parents' house was always full of strange Europeans, refugees who were fed, clothed, and treated as family.

Now the astonishing relief in my body and spirit told me of the unknown burden I had carried. I had visited Jean to expose her, not to get a message from my dead grandmother. Yet through Jean it had happened, and somehow a release had occurred. I had been released from the unrecognized fear and guilt from my grandmother's death. I wanted to bounce, leap, dance—do something to express the elation I felt. The rest of the hour passed quickly, and Jean handed me a tape of the reading, suggested a list of books I might read, and also suggested I pay close attention to my dreams.

After Helen's reading, we drove home, fixed tea, and listened to each other's tapes. Jean had spoken to Helen of the major surgery Helen had had some ten years before and of her past lives, showing her how incidents and issues had arisen in them which seemed to connect with her current experiences.

"Isn't that fascinating, Pecki!" Helen said. "What's next?"

That night, Paul and I went to my mother's apartment to see her visiting cousin, Sylvia, a small, chic, smiling woman, whom neither of us had met before. After some small talk, I said, (leaving psychics out of it), "Mom, I had a dream about Grandmother Zorn last night."

"I've got goosebumps all over," said my mother.

"People always say I look like your grandmother," said Sylvia. "It must be my size. We're both small."

"But you're smiling," I said. "I don't remember Grandmother Zorn ever smiling. Would you describe her for me as you remember her, Sylvia?"

And, in the same body language as Jean's, Sylvia straightened her back, swept the hair from her forehead to the back of her neck, indicating a bun, and took on my dead grandmother's appearance. My heart pounding, I pinched Paul to make sure that he was paying attention. Sylvia was saying, "She was aristocratic, you know, regal and distant. I was afraid of her."

My mother joined in with stories of Grandmother Zorn: her gardens, her pansies, and how she loved their little faces. "She was able to talk her sick plants back to health, you know."

"Did you see that, Paul? Did you see Sylvia? She did and said the same things about Grandmother that Jean Quinn did. And. . . and Jean repeated to me what I said to you this morning," I told him as soon as we got into the car.

Once home, I insisted that Paul listen to the tape.

Losing the burden of guilt I had unknowingly been carrying energized me for weeks after that. My daily routines no longer bothered me. All the driving I had to do — to school, Little League, music lessons, etc. — was no longer a burden. I smiled and laughed more easily, ran, even skipped. And Paul said, "I'm a pragmatist, so whether or not Jean Hastings Quinn has psychic powers doesn't matter. I can acknowledge what I see: the difference in you."

Chapter 3

Yellow Tulips

I determined that there would continue to be a difference: a difference in my health, attitude, and their impact on my family's well being. If I could find programs which would help me, which might lead me to strength and health and self-development, I was going to try to follow them. Jean Quinn had suggested I pay attention to my dreams and a few days later I read in the local paper that there was a dream workshop being conducted at the Creutzberg Center, $40.00 for 12 two-hour classes.

I was a constant dreamer, even though I couldn't make heads or tails out of their storyline. If I told my dreams to Paul, he interpreted them according to Freud, and his interpretations made me very uncomfortable.

"Oh, Paul, bug off," I would say after he talked about my penis envy.

"Do you know that one of the magazines sent out a survey asking women if they'd rather have a penis or a fur coat, Paul, and 90% of them chose the fur coat? Penis envy, baloney—but I love yours anyway," I said one morning. (Paul, however, was already late to work.)

Because of my discomfort with those Freudian interpretations, I called the instructor, Marianne Wolf, to ask about the dream workshop.

"What did you say your name was?" Marianne asked. "I don't think I'm catching it. What? We must have a bad connection."

"Pecki Sherman. P-E-C-K-I," I spelled, thinking that the nickname given to me by my father (he called me his "Tzvaita Pekel," his second package) was unclear.

"Will you give me your address and phone number, Pecki? Just in case."

"I'll give you my new address because we're moving. It's Sporting Hill Farm on Mountain Top Road."

There was a pause long enough to make me wonder if we'd been cut off, and then Marianne Wolf said quite clearly, "I wonder if you could come to my house this afternoon."

I thought quickly. "Yes, yes, I can." The boys were spending the afternoon with friends. And suddenly that electricity was there, the same electricity associated with Grandmother Zorn.

As we were sitting in the living room of Marianne's country house, I told her about Grandmother Zorn and Jean Hastings Quinn. The afternoon sunlight streaming through the blue and white colonial glass collection in the windows made rainbows here and there throughout the room. One rainbow spread out on my lap, another lay on Marianne's soft white hair and picked up the bright blue of her eyes in a curve of colors. "I've been expecting you. I didn't know who it was I was expecting, but when you called, I knew it was you."

I forgot to sip the fresh darjeeling tea Marianne had poured from her tall Wedgewood pot into its matching white and blue teacups.

"But why were you expecting me?"

"Because of a dream I had last night. It took place in a doctor's office—a place of healing. Two people there were having a conversation about a journey and I joined in. The substance of it was that I was to go with them. Then we were at a railroad station. I was on one platform and one of my dream acquaintances was on the other, across the tracks. We were yelling our names and addresses back and forth, and it was very difficult to hear. The name wasn't Pecki Sherman, but it was a name that I couldn't get. And in the dream a mountain appeared, so when you said that you lived on Mountain Top Road, I knew you were someone I should meet."

Of course I signed up for the class Marianne was giving. It would be a good first step in getting to know myself. There were ten women in it, and not one seemed exotic. They were like the people you see in a supermarket.

One woman told of a dream in which she felt that she must go home but was unable to, since the horse on which she was riding proceeded in another direction. She tried to turn him, yanked at the reins to pull his head around, kicked him in the flank to turn his hindquarters, but to no avail. He continued in his own direction, and she became more and more fearful, particularly as a large stone wall loomed ahead and the horse was galloping towards it. She woke up trembling and dripping with sweat.

In class discussion led by Marianne, we were told to depersonalize the characters (both horse and rider) and break the dream into segments, such as:

1. Someone had to go home.
2. Someone was going in the wrong direction.
3. Someone could not force a change in direction.
4. Someone was heading for a crash.

"It looks as if my dream had two themes, one's loss of control, and the other's that events in my life are running away with me."

"Do you want to do anything to change the situation?"
"Yes."
"Well, what are your options?"
And the dreamer listed those she saw.

Marianne stressed to the class the need for the dreamer to work out for herself her dream themes. She must also feel comfortable with the interpretation. When theme and interpretation become clear, the dreamer begins to realize her options. "You'll know it's right when you feel your own 'ah-ha,'" said Marianne.

On my way to the third meeting of the dream class, a nagging thought began to rap in my head. "Buy tulips for Marianne." Nonsense, I'm already late, and tulips aren't in season. But the words began to pound — go buy tulips, go buy tulips, go buy tulips — until, feeling thoroughly annoyed and not a little foolish, I stopped at the Farmer's Market and, among masses of flowers at a back booth, I found a dozen yellow tulips. When I arrived in class, Marianne was saying that she felt sick and had almost not come. Then she saw the flowers.

"How did you know, Pecki?"

"Know what?"

"That I needed yellow tulips?"

"Why?" asked someone in the class.

"Some years ago, I was recovering from a heart attack, and I dreamt of a building, a church-like building that had two large planters outside filled with yellow tulips. Yellow is a color that, for me, represents healing. In my dream, those tulips spoke to me of cleansing and a return to health. Since that time, whenever I'm not quite well, I think of those yellow tulips and I seem to feel better. I already feel better having them on my desk, Pecki. Thank you."

The overwhelming pounding in my head had been for a reason. I had been right to listen to it. It had been far more than a whim, but I said to the others, "It was a coincidence."

"Not a coincidence, but synchronicity," Marianne said.

Synchronicity? Did that explain the coincidences that were piling up quite alarmingly?

"Synchronicity is a coincidence that could be called purposeful — coincidental events which are significant to us and cannot be explained away. Learn to recognize them and allow them to happen in your life. . . Now let's begin writing down our dreams."

In the beginning, we new students found that difficult, but we practiced remembering our dreams and, upon awakening, writing them down — even if only fragments — a word, a scene, a feeling. As we became better able to recall their content, we began to establish a theme or themes, keeping in mind Marianne's advice that most dreams deal with events in our daily lives. The first step, she said, in finding out what advice a dream is giving you is to look at the whole dream and to ask yourself what's going on. The second step is to depersonalize the characters. (You become Someone. Someone is angry. Someone is being threatened by someone else.) And the third step is to look for connections between the dream and what is happening in your daily life. After these steps in a first round of analysis are taken, symbols are examined.

"Begin with an unabridged dictionary," Marianne said. "All the words in a dream and all their meanings are important. Look at the definitions. One may be just right. You'll get the 'ah-ha' that will tell you so, and you'll know that's the right interpretation for you. Look for humor and puns, too."

"Like my horse running away," said the woman who had had the horse dream.

"Exactly. Try to remember colors and remember how you feel when you wake up. Is it a good feeling or a bad feeling? What do the symbols in your dream mean to you?"

"In my dream there was a bed and I felt good about it. It was a good symbol. It seemed to mean safety—some kind of security," said one person.

"Security in *my* dreams seems to be represented by food."

"When there's a man in my dreams, he seems to represent authority," said a third.

"In my dreams, authority is represented by a nun. I went to Catholic school, and, in my dreams, I have to do what those nuns say."

"Have you considered saying no to them?" Marianne asked. "Taking authority for your own life?"

"I think I would feel better if I did."

At the next session, the student reported that she had said no to the nun in her dream and had awakened feeling happy.

Some of the dreams the women in the class had seemed to be warnings. The night before a job interview one woman dreamed that the interview was to take place in a moving automobile. When she went for the actual interview, she discovered that the job bore no relation to the one she had applied for. She realized that she had been "taken for a ride" in both the dream and in reality.

"Now I'm beginning to understand the nightmares I had as a child," I said during one class. "When I was a child, my parents were always telling stories of the horrors in concentration camps and of war and famine, and I had terrible dreams. Later, in 1961, during the Cuban crisis, my younger brother had a full cast on his leg because of a bone-cartilage weakness, and I dreamt that the Pied Piper had come to town to save the children, but my brother couldn't make it to safety. I was terrified in the dream that he would not make it to the safety of the mountain and be destroyed. It's clear it had something to do with all my childhood fears."

It was also clear that we all were learning to listen to and understand important messages from our subconsciouses. We were learning a language previously hidden, but the meanings of that language were only our own. It was our own 'ah-ha,' as Marianne said, that translated the dream.

"I read that if you sleep with your head to the north when the moon is full, you remember your dreams better, Paul," I said one full-moon night. "Let's move our bed."

"Do you know how much work that is? Anyway, it won't fit."

"Well, we'll sleep sideways, then."

"Not me. I won't.

"All right, I'll sleep on the floor."

"Ok, ok, we'll sleep sideways."

We turned the bedding and settled down. I worried that Paul might be uncomfortable since his feet hung over the edge of the bed, but mostly, I envisioned the wonderful dream I was going to have. However, I could not remember a dream when Paul woke me at six a.m. "Listen," he said, "I had this incredible dream. I was in this huge ocean. Magnificent fish. It seemed like an aquarium because part of it was behind glass. I was participant and observer at the same time, and in front of me was a control panel with buttons I could push. I controlled the ocean, but I was the ocean. It was super. Those fish! The colors, the currents, I can't get over it."

"And you don't even like to swim, Paul."

"But there it was. I had that dream, and I loved it."

"Well, what do you think it meant?"

He gave me a delighted smile and jumped into his morning shower.

Up until then, he'd been making a bit of fun about what I was doing, but he had that dream, and, later in the day, he found himself telling a group of businessmen about it. "You know my wife made me do the craziest thing last night, and I had this dream. . ." His ocean was the first happy dream he remembered.

After that, Paul gave me the affirmation I needed from him. He acquiesced in my interpretation of my own dreams and forgot about Freud. In their turn, my dreams focused on matters I must pay attention to: mostly on my past and my childhood fears about war and separation. The symbols occasionally changed, but the themes remained constant. And the little internal 'ah-ha' I felt interpreted the symbols for me as efficiently as if I were Pharaoh and had my own Joseph inside.

A week or so later, I found a rabbi with a coat of many colors. I had been looking for Jewish guidance, anxious to follow my good electricity in a Jewish way, if possible. I noticed that when the electricity was flowing, I had warmth in my constantly cold right hand, its circulation having been impeded by a tennis injury no doctor seemed able to correct. I had no intention of stopping the electricity which seemed to be responsible for that improvement. I wanted, if possible, to see what could be done for the radiating pain in my elbow, for headaches that were sinus and allergy-related, even for my painful, irregular menstrual cycle. But was it all right with my God?

I heard about a rabbi who taught philosophy and religion at a local university. Reb Zalman Schacter-Shalomi was at the forefront of a contemporary renewal of Jewish spirituality, I learned from an article in a local newspaper. It seemed that he was presenting the central teachings of Hassidism and Kabbalah in a new way. He seemed the right authority for me to consult.

The respected Rabbi and well-known professor opened the door of his office to me with a cordial welcome and a strong radiant presence that dominated the cluttered room. His round face was surrounded by bushy hair and a graying bushy beard. His round body was dressed in colorful rumpled clothes.

Before we could start talking, the telephone rang. The Rabbi made a dash for the desk, scattered some papers on the floor, ran to the nearby bookcase and pushed aside mounds of books stacked every which way. While the phone increased in stridency, the Rabbi dashed around his office, pulling at his bushy beard and saying, "Wait a minute, wait a minute, I'm coming. The phone, the phone, where did I put it," to finally follow the cord which I saw leading beneath his desk. By the time he answered, there was no one on the line, and the Rabbi turned to me with a little shrug.

"So now what can I do for you?"

"Rabbi, can I tell you about seeing a psychic and some electricity that I'm feeling and about my grandmother?"

"Let me hear." He settled back, folded his arms, and looked at me in a comforting manner, while I plunged into the visit with Jean Quinn, "and then the electricity in my body started. She described my grandmother exactly."

"How much did she charge you?" the Rabbi asked.

"Twenty-six dollars."

"Twenty-six. It's a good number. It's a good price," he said, nodding his head. (A few years later I learned that the number 26 represents YHVH, the true name of God, in

Kabbalah numerology.)

"Learn how to use your electricity, Pecki. Use it to heal. Teach your hands and your heart healing. Take an introductory course in Therapeutic Touch."

"What's Therapeutic Touch?"

"It's one of the methods used for healing with energy. It's related to the ancient practice of the laying on of hands."

As he said those words, I felt my good electricity tingle in the center of my palms. I had found my Jewish confirmation and he had shown me the next step.

I thanked him. As I left, the Rabbi said "Come back whenever you like, we can talk some more."

Jean Hastings Quinn, Marianne Wolf, and now Reb Zalman had all been on my path, a path that led to New York University and a three-day introductory course in Therapeutic Touch. Paul said, "Off on another tangent, Pecki? Well, the course description sounds interesting."

Chapter 4

Pan's Music

When I told my mother I was taking a long weekend course at the School of Nursing at NYU, my mother said, "What's wrong with a hospital here? My training was excellent, and that way you can be at home in the evening . . . Who's gonna make a dinner for Paul, Pecki?"

"There's nowhere in the city that I know of to take the course, Mom. And Paul will be just fine. He and the boys know how to use a can opener."

"Therapeutic Touch? What's that, anyway?"

"It has something to do with healing and it only costs $60.00. Helen and I will be going together."

"Oh. At least you're not going alone, then."

Helen and I took the train to New York and a bus to Greenwich Village. Washington Square was so littered with newspapers and bums that even the grass had been worn away by bodies sleeping on it. We had to thread through a bunch of spaced-out people to get to the building where the course was being held. Helen was happy to be back in New York, the city of her youth, but I didn't like the grungy neighborhood or the gasoline fumes suffusing the air.

The classroom was airless and dingy, our instructor was six feet tall. She swished in in a purple cape and began to describe the uses of Therapeutic Touch in a hospital setting.

"Therapeutic Touch is practiced by many of our nurses here. How many of this group are in the medical professions?"

Half of the sixteen students raised their hands.

"Therapeutic Touch is a method of channelling human energy through the hands to help someone who is ill either physically or emotionally. It involves learning to center one-self — that is, reach deeply within — becoming aware of one's inner self and bringing one's energy field into alignment with another's."

Helen and I looked at each other and shrugged our shoulders at the unfamiliar terms. The instructor smiled at us.

"You'll understand what I'm talking about when we begin the exercises."

"For the first exercise, hold your hands two inches apart. Now move them away from each other about six inches, then towards each other again, then away, slowly, until you begin to feel a substance in the space between your hands."

"It feels elastic."

"Sort of gummy."

"I can feel the pull."

"My hands feel tingly."

"It's warm there."

"I don't feel anything," said the man near Helen.

"Helen, put your hands around his. Your energy field will stimulate his energy field."

Helen moved her hands around the hands of the man and a slow smile spread across his face. "I feel it, I feel it."

"Does anyone in the class have a minor ailment?" the teacher asked.

"Well, I have a headache," said one of the women.

The teacher bounced her hands about eighteen inches away from both sides of the student's head. "I can feel your headache. It's way out here." She measured and made a slow, smooth, combing motion through the air around the student's head and shoulders. After a moment or so, the class could see tension leaving the student's face as the teacher's hands moved closer to her head.

"That's wonderful. I feel as if you've pulled my headache away."

"Now I'm unruffling your energy field," said the teacher, moving her hands down the space beside the student's body and toward the floor.

"What does it mean, unruffling your energy field?" I asked.

"Find a partner and you'll feel it for yourself."

The first step was for the partners to pat their "energy balls" between their hands by moving the palms apart and together as the teacher had demonstrated. Then my partner, one of the nurses, working from the top of my head, moved her hands down the front of my body. "I feel it. I feel something bumpy. It must be your energy field, Pecki."

"The bumps come from an uneven distribution of energy," the teacher explained.

"Why do I feel such a strong energy around Pecki's right shoulder and arm?" asked the nurse. "It almost pushes my hand away."

"Have you ever had an injury there, Pecki?"

"A bad tennis injury, and I've had years of cortisone shots in my shoulder and elbow to get rid of this radiating pain."

"Smooth out the field in that area. Pull it down through Pecki's fingers. That's right. Now throw it off."

I felt as if a powerful stream of water was hosing out my arm from shoulder to fingers, as if a kind of dam was being washed out and whatever the dam had been blocking washed away.

I felt a release from pain that I had never experienced during or after the many medical treatments of my arm, administered by different doctors in the different places Paul and I had lived. How come, I thought to myself, a movement of somebody's hands around my body, not even touching it, could relieve the pain I've had in that arm for almost fifteen years—before the kids were born, even. Just hands passing my body in the air could remove pain from my arm? So simple and yet effective. It's not logical. It's almost a miracle — but I'm not questioning it.

For the rest of the course, we learned to unruffle, release and direct the body energy, that electricity which I had already experienced as "good", which flowed from an energy field that we were learning to identify and direct. This introductory course was not preparing us to heal other people but was putting us in touch with a force we had always possessed and been completely unaware of, a force that all people possess, a force we could use for our own good, the teacher assured us.

To the present day, the pain in my shoulder has not returned. The release of that painful physical condition told me that the energy I experienced at NYU, my electricity, wasn't solely of an emotional or mental origin. What I had been learning and was determined to continue to learn had connections with physical, spiritual and mental aspects of myself and with forces outside of me too. There was a connectedness operating. How else to put it? I had felt it in my garden, felt it the first time I touched my knees to the soil and planted my first bulb. I was already 28 when that happened (was not yet ecologically aware, did not know that the purity of our air depended upon the equatorial rain forests, for instance), but I was coming to know the strength of the connection between myself and the earthworm beside my trowel. We had more in common than the soil we were both working. We were part of a linked and extended world. We were in a partnership that required the right work from both of us in the service of the great power of nature.

In the 19th century, the American Indian, Red Bird, said, "We believe that there is a mysterious power, greater than all others, which is represented in nature, one form being the sun." Through my knees on the earth I had felt that power, felt it too through my good electricity and through the message from my grandmother. The new awareness was unblocking many areas of myself, areas in which I was arrogant, skeptical, inflexible, and ignorant, but in which I felt now a possibility for change. I was ready to put care and respect and effort into making changes in my life, changes that would put me in sync with a natural life, changes that would come from both my waking and dreaming selves. On returning home I found that out.

It was summer. I was nineteen and walking on a busy street in war-torn Europe. He was too handsome, too healthy, too strong-looking for the Gestapo to pass him by, I thought. But somehow he was still alive. He took me by the arm and walked me through battered and bombed-out streets, out of the town, into a deep forest.

They were a gathering of partisans, meeting in the woods to plan strategies of escape for those about to be seized by the Nazis.

The forest was cool, shaded by tall evergreens, carpeted by ferns and moss. Occasional sunlight filtering through the trees struck a nearby stream, and became a spray of diamonds.

The group was small, ten people who had managed to survive, to form a network for transporting families through the area — a hundred families in the next month — but there weren't enough secure hiding places, food, or clothing. I was chattering with fear at the enormity of the task.

He took my hand and pulled me away from the group to the mossy lap of a giant tree. The roots ran over the ground like great arms before disappearing into the earth, and seemed to hug us as we nestled down. The sound of the brook, the comfort of the tree, and the security of tall ferns which hid us from sight began to calm me.

We sat quietly for a while, then he leaned forward, loosed a giant bulbous root from the ground, a root like a Jerusalem artichoke, held it tenderly in his hands and blew into it. I had never heard a sound so magical, mystical, celestial. I sat transfixed, realizing that there was no instrument that had such a range. Pan's pipes! I felt my heart beat faster and faster, my body get hotter. I burned with love and joy. But the heat grew so intense that I felt I could no longer stand it, and woke up, realizing that it was a dream.

I tried to get back into the dream, not wanting to lose the man, my hero, comforter, lover. But even more than him, I wanted to keep the music from the Jerusalem artichoke.

And later I learned that Yogis were familiar with the experience of hearing music of inconceivable beauty emanating from no apparent source. This phenomenon was called "Nad" in Sanskrit. In Jewish history, the same phenomenon was called "celestial music" by the Kabbalists.

It carried me for weeks, that music, turning me into a kind of walking, living joy, the same joy I had felt when I had been released from the guilt of my grandmother's suicide. Each step in my new education, from my session with Jean Quinn to the course in Therapeutic Touch, was adding to that. I felt electric enough and powerful enough to be able to heal the world by touching it. But I lacked the nerve to try.

One day I saw a dog that had been struck by a car lying beside the road. I wanted to stop, barge through the crowd around it, spread out my hands, and heal its bloody body. But there was a policeman in charge, and the people there would think I was crazy, and there was so much more for me to learn before I could feel sure of my ability to heal that I drove on. I reminded myself that even though I could not yet use my good electricity to heal others, the power and joy were there, and part of it came from my dream of the handsome young partisan blowing through the Jerusalem artichoke. My Jewish roots. The music had released me from the fear, panic, and crisis orientation which formed the background of the dream, and which I had thought was my Jewish background, that background which in my family had focused on what had happened to Nazi victims during the thirties and forties. I was born in 1939 during my family's effort to help the persecuted.

Dad worked as a printer, Mom as a nurse. There was just enough money to support three children and aid grandparents, but what there was was shared with visitors passing through Philadelphia. Our home was referred to as the Bail-in Hotel, since so many scholars, artists, musicians, and politicians stopped there. Conversation went on late into the night and we children were allowed to participate. When we fell asleep, our Bubba put us to bed.

Actors were frequently guests as well, and my father saw to it that we went to the theatre, particularly the Lincoln Theatre where the plays were in Yiddish, trading his printing for seats in the manager's box.

When I was a skinny seven-year-old, I acted the part of a little girl released from a concentration camp at the end of the Second World War. Because I was thin and owned an appropriate dress and could speak Yiddish, and because my father was known to many of the actors who stayed at our house, I was given the child lead. Menasha Skulnick, the famous comedian, was the star. I almost closed down the play one night by running on stage in the first act, so nervous from having seen both my grandmothers sitting in the fifth row that I mistakenly recited my lines of the last act's final scene and gave away the plot, which concerned the discovery of my lost father in the person of the handsome, mustachioed leading man. The producer was so dismayed that he dropped the curtain on the play and had to be persuaded to let it go on again. Quite understandably, I was not invited to continue with the show to New York, but my Bubba told me "du bist di besta aktrissa oif der Yiddisher bina": I was the best actress on the Jewish stage.

Like more than one Jewish girl of the time, I identified with Anna Frank, and, when I was eighteen, auditioned to play her part on the stage. I was sure that under other circumstances I would have been Anna's best friend. I appeared for the audition in my favorite soft white leather jacket and cord skirt, but was dismissed by the director as looking too collegiate. Susan Strasburg got the part.

My dream of Pan's music showed me that my background held more than victims. It was rooted in beautiful sounds, enveloped in love and joy. My parents had been able to find joy in what they did with their lives. It was only I who had not been aware of that.

Now I was becoming aware of the richness of my heritage and the resources around and within me that could help me in my everyday life, both with emotional trauma and physical pain. To get to those resources I would have to assume a new kind of responsibility, however, not the kind of responsibility that lived up to other people's expectations — the responsibility of good wife, good mother, good citizen — but the kind of responsibility which would be self-evaluating and self-motivating, which would lead me to what I thought would be fulfillment.

Chapter 5

Sporting Hill Farm

In the past, some ways of fulfillment had not been easy. In particular, I had not been able to conceive a child.

When Paul decided that it was time to have a family, I had a few doubts because of my history of irregular menstrual cycles, which for years had been treated without avail, but I wasn't really worried.

After months of trying to conceive, I decided to visit the gynecologist. He suggested a D&C (dusting and cleaning, a doctor's joke). At the hospital, I was prepared, given a shot, and wheeled into the operating room. "Is this a clinic patient?" one of the nurses asked as I was being lifted onto the operating table. My God, I thought, they'll cut off one of my legs. "I'm not a clinic patient," I tried to tell them, but no sound came out of my mouth. Instead, I began to shake so severely that I felt my teeth rattling, and the medical staff was obliged to re-anesthetize me twice in order to stop it. The ten minute procedure took three hours to perform.

Then, a year later I was in the hospital to have my Fallopian tubes blown open. (It was discovered that they were already.)

On a monthly basis I was flat on my back, naked from the waist down, with my feet in the stirrups at the gynecologist's. I was given medication to keep my hormonal clock ticking properly, and admonished to prepare accurate temperature charts. I was not ovulating on a regular basis, and, therefore, could not conceive, the doctor said. His answer was medication that would keep the hands of my hormonal clock running on time. Also, I was not trying enough, so he said. The doctor sat behind his big desk in his big swivel chair surrounded with pictures of all the newborns he had brought into the world. I stared at the portrait of his wife and his kids smiling through their braces, shrank into my chair, and said, "Yes." Yes, I would take my temperature, keep an accurate chart, take my medicine, see him next month, thank you. But I stopped wearing clean underpants when I went to his office.

And my anger built up.

Then it was Paul's turn. He had to take a sperm test. He was put into a little room and told to produce a sample, after which he was instructed to arrange himself on hands and knees on the doctor's table while various instruments were clamped to his private parts and he was poked and prodded by the proctologist. The room had four doors and Paul swore that the nurses walked by, looked in, and laughed. His test results guaranteed that he could impregnate half the world, but the experience shook him up so much that he told me I need never go to the gynecologist again. We decided to adopt a child, and I determined to give up my job teaching first grade.

Like a miracle, we were offered a five-day-old boy.

He was beautiful—and hungry every two hours. He burped and smiled at the same time. He turned his little head and looked at each of us as we talked to him, and, of course, we thought he was a genius.

We called him Joshua for the Joshua who fought the battle of Jericho, who was second in command to Moses, and who spoke to the sun and moon. Our new baby represented to us the "promised land."

The next year when the adoption was to be finalized, we took Josh to Family Court. He was dressed in blue flannel suspender shorts and navy knee socks which exposed knees as round and rosy as his cheeks. He had on a white shirt under his blue checked jacket, and his blond hair, which I had carefully brushed back, lay in moist curls on his forehead. He looked around at the people in the judge's chamber and at the judge herself with wide brown eyes. At fifteen months he was already talking (see, a genius, just as I'd thought), and when the judge took him on her lap and asked him, "Where are your mommy and your daddy, Josh?" he looked at her in astonishment, pointed at us, and said in his baby voice, "There Josh mommy. There daddy, too," climbed down from her lap, and ran to hug me around the legs.

"There's no question about this adoption," said the judge. "You can sign the papers now."

That year and the next were particularly joyous. We had our little Josh, and with the help of the gynecologist and his medication that kept my clock ticking, I conceived and in nine months delivered our second son.

Jonathan, named for my special grandfather, was born smiling. With two babies, I became content to stay home, plant a garden, adopt puppies and kittens, and follow Paul up the corporate ladder. That involved several moves, moves connected to promotions, opportunities, and improved economic situations. I was the one who made all the moves bearable, found the right house with the right school and kids nearby. Wherever Paul's business success led us, we went. From state to state and town to town, following a father-knows-best pattern. The last move in our nineteen years of marriage was to Sporting Hill Farm. This was a move for ourselves, to a place in the country, close to Paul's work, with a court for his tennis, a barn for a pony or horse for the boys, and a garden for me.

Sporting Hill Farm had a two-hundred-year-old farmhouse on seven rolling acres, two barns, and a tool shed that looked like the guardhouse at Buckingham Palace. The main house had a cedar roof covered with British Soldier moss which, after a rain, sprouted "red helmets," thick walls of plastered fieldstone, and old windows of six-over-nine leaded glass panes.

Over the years, there had been additions to the house, so that old pine floors abutted new oak ones and two feet deep window sills elbowed cushioned bays. Early American and Spanish architecture were laid cheek by jowl, and somehow didn't rub each other the wrong way.

The property had been an old hunt club, so the fields were fenced and there were dog kennels and runs. There were sixty-foot shade trees, fruit trees, grape vines, and black currant bushes. There were boxwoods fifteen feet high. The view to the north was over a valley. There was a swimming pool, friends for the kids a short drive away, and Paul's office within eight minutes. We were going to be gentlemen farmers. Paul and I laughed at ourselves, but knew how lucky we were.

We moved in May when Josh was thirteen and Jonathan eleven. The late bulbs were blooming, apples and cherries shot cannonades of blossom, and twenty fragrant lilac bushes bombarded our noses. Sixer immediately dug up the nearest neighbor's garden.

Paul got a shiny green John Deere tractor. For his Bar Mitzvah, we bought Josh a Labrador puppy, whom he named Sunshine, and whom he loved so much that he invited her to share his bed at night and took over her complete care, including feeding and housebreaking. In time, he taught her to roll over, fetch, sit up, and shake hands. At a sheriff's sale later in the summer, we bought Prince, a Palomino, abandoned and left to starve when his previous owners divorced each other and moved away. Prince was given to Jonathan who fixed up a cozy stall for him in the barn and set about a program of fattening him up. Jonathan got up every morning at 6:00 a.m. to feed Prince before going off to school. Prince was big, and Paul and I were a little afraid of him, but, as he recovered strength and gentleness from good care, we lost our fear and began to love him, and, since he wouldn't be happy alone in the barn, we took in another horse as a boarder. A kitten, whom we named Tenzing after Hillary's companion, came next. He lived up to his name by attacking — instead of Mt. Everest — every tall tree in sight.

For Paul's birthday, I bought two goats, Gilda and Radner. Since it was February, they lived in the kitchen and have ever since jumped over fences to knock at the back door.

We enjoyed food from my organic garden that first summer on the farm. The boys and their friends picked apples, cherries, currants, raspberries, and peaches. We all planted seven long rows of potatoes and more rows of peas, beans, beets, and lettuce. We weeded and hoed, and the boys, under Paul's supervision, drove the green tractor and its red wagon across the fields. In spite of the work that everyone had to do, Sporting Hill Farm offered a serenity that brought more and more visitors there to share our dinner from the garden and to sit around the kitchen table talking into the night.

On hot days during that summer, we often had friends come to the farm to swim in our pool as well. I was not a good swimmer, but Josh undertook to teach me. He had been swimming since he was five, and, as he did in all sports, handled himself well. But he had a problem getting me to cooperate. I didn't like that cold deep water.

"Now, Mommy, come on. Get in the water."

"I've already had a swim, Josh."

"That wasn't a swim. You just dunked. We'll just swim to the end and back. I'll be with you. It's easy. Come on, Mom."

And so he would argue me into the water and urge me until I'd swum the length of the pool. Sunshine often dove in to join us, and Josh would have to protect me from her claws.

At the end of the summer, the children were a bit apprehensive about going to a new school. "I don't know what you boys are nervous about," I told them. "You've already met some of the kids in the neighborhood, and you both make friends easily. That won't be a problem. And as for the work, you know your grades have always been good: all A's and B's last report, Josh. Stop worrying." That seemed to help a little, and they went off on the school bus one warm September morning cheerily enough.

Left to myself, I felt less than cheery about the amount of work to be done. I had a large house to care for, a lot of errands to do, animals to provide for, and an overflowing harvest in the garden to somehow use. I realized that I must have some help. I advertised in the local paper for a part-time housekeeper, and Emma Jean Weaver responded.

"I can't come to see you today, Mrs. Sherman. I'm waiting for my bread to rise."

"Oh, you bake bread?"

"Every week. Today I have ten loaves. There's three men in the family."

"Are you going to have time to help me, then?" I liked her voice and she baked bread. It seemed to me that I already tasted melted butter on its pungent yeasty insides.

"Oh yes, I'll have time. My canning's finished for the year."

And I had never canned in my life.

Emma Jean appeared the next day—a short, robust woman with a smile from ear to ear. She walked into the house, looked around, and asked to see the garden.

"We'd better can these tomatoes tomorrow, Mrs. Sherman."

"Well, uh, there aren't any jars". . .

"I'll bring what we need," said Emma Jean, and I had a wonderful feeling of being taken care of.

As we worked on the tomatoes the next day, slipping off skins of those that had been dunked in hot water, Emma Jean told me about growing up on a one-acre farm where her Dunkard family raised hogs and chickens and grew all the vegetables they needed for the year. "We kids used to make furrows by dragging the plow behind us, after our papa had paid a neighbor two dollars a day to cultivate the ground with his mule.

"My papa worked for the railroad, and Mamma and we kids did berry picking when the raspberries and blackberries were in. We got paid five cents a quart. One day I only made twenty-five cents, but then I ate most of them. . . You should make cider and vinegar out of all those apples in the orchard, Mrs. Sherman. Otherwise, what a waste. Cider's mighty good, but for vinegar you need a mother."

"A mother?"

"To start it—like yeast or yogurt, you know. We used to make two barrels of cider and one of vinegar for the winter. Picked our apples at Nicodemus's Orchards. Windfalls, of course."

"Did you ever play, Emma Jean?"

"Busy hands make short work, our mamma used to say, but yes, there was time for play, also."

As the fall progressed, the busy hands of Emma Jean taught me to bake a variety of breads and cakes, to make crabapple jelly and raspberry jam as well as to can the remains of the garden. I noticed that there was an increasing number of visiting children on the days that Emma Jean was baking bread or cookies or cinnamon buns. She did most of the work, but she gave me the credit.

"Did you bake these buns, Emma Jean?" Paul would ask as he came into the fragrant cinnamony kitchen, and Emma Jean would answer, "I helped Pecki bake them."

"My wife is a woman of many talents," Paul would say, winking at me, while he helped himself to a syrupy, plumply-raisined bun.

Cooking the produce of my gardens, working in the last burst of beans and pumpkins while feeling the sun on my skin, the earth under my feet, a communion with all the life around me, from Sixer to the red fox in the woods, made me want to celebrate the ancient festival of Sukkot. I suggested to the family that we build a Sukkah, a temporary outdoor room or shed leaning against the house which is used as a dining room for seven days at harvest time in order to thank God for the crops.

Paul and the boys bought ten two-by-fours, and we constructed its frame on our terrace, making walls of corn stalks, and decorating with leaves, grapes, and popcorn strung from the timbers. On the roof of the Sukkah, we laid boughs of evergreens, making sure to leave spaces for seeing the stars at night. During the seven days of Sukkot, we ate there, inviting our friends to join us, and, for me at least, establishing a new connectedness to the heavens and earth.

One night Emma Jean and her family joined us, bringing the best cakes I've ever tasted. "Because of farm eggs," she said. "Fresh eggs make better baking." That was all the encouragement I needed to fix up the kennels for chickens. We cleared the dog runs, laid lots of sawdust, set up laying boxes and perches, and had a chicken house for ten white Leghorns, ten Rhode Island Reds, and a proud Banty rooster with his own Banty hen. We used milk glass eggs to encourage the hens to lay.

Unfortunately, Sixer enjoyed catching chickens and shaking them by the neck. Several unlucky ones fell victim to him. To keep Sixer out of the henhouse, whoever was feeding had to slip through the door very fast indeed — not such an easy thing to do with a pail of water to carry going in and a dozen or so eggs coming out. However, I managed, and Sixer, often accompanied by tag-along Sunshine, was obliged to do his plotting outside of the chicken house, while the chickens pecked and clucked in their safe wire runs.

As the year drew to a close, I was so contented at Sporting Hill Farm that I could have clucked too. I felt that I never wanted to leave what seemed to be a perfect environment, one that provided not only a safe, simple, and healthy life for my children, but a serene and enriching one for Paul and me. When I was loving my family and animals, feeding the birds, working in my garden, I seemed to be following my "good electricity." I felt that everything around me was good and right and I was living in joy. I was living the old Shaker song:

'Tis a gift to be simple. 'Tis a gift to be free.
'Tis a gift to come round where we ought to be.
And when we are in the place just right
We'll be in the valley of love and delight.

Chapter 6

Lakes of the Clouds

During our second summer, while Sixer and Sunshine were busy watching chickens, Paul playing tennis, and Emma Jean and I baking pull-apart cinnamon buns, a canker was growing.

In spite of the fact that Sporting Hill Farm seemed to be therapeutic to family and friends alike, who would often come looking for work to do, for a chance to get their hands into the soil perhaps or to drive the tractor over the fields, there was something destructive developing in our idyllic scene.

While Henrietta Chicken, our Rhode Island Red, was being persecuted by the Leghorns, Josh was persecuting Jonathan.

In Henrietta's case, we solved the problem by moving her from the chicken coop to the goats' wire enclosed stall in the barn. Jonathan, our twelve-year-old barn boy, was excellent with all animals—including Henrietta—and, under his care in the safety of the goats' stall, that lady soon regrew her plucked-out feathers and resurrected her bedraggled comb. She began laying beautiful brown eggs again and was almost ready to move back to the chicken coop when one day, while Jonathan and his friend Matt were cleaning the barn, Henrietta escaped from her stall, Sixer sneaked in, and a chase ensued. Henrietta flew onto a rafter, Sixer vaulted up beside her and grabbed her in his jaws. There was a terrible panicky squawking from Henrietta while Jonathan and Matt tried to grab her from Sixer, who ran between their legs and out into the field, Henrietta dangling from his mouth and Sunshine yapping behind him. That, of course, was the end of her. But, since she was so much a part of the family, Jonathan didn't tell me then how she died.

Nor did he tell me he was being picked on by Josh. Josh would tell Jonathan he was small and skinny and a wimp and besides his friends were creeps — which sounds fairly normal dialogue for sibling rivals, and I took it as such. But Josh would also push his brother around, a punch here, a dig there, a knocking of Jonathan off his feet, leaving a residue of unease and unpleasantness in my mind, which was amplified by the behavior of Josh's new friends, the older brothers and sisters of kids his own age.

Those sixteen to eighteen-year-olds were driving cars, motorcycles, and motorbikes, and Josh wanted to do the same, of course. But he was only fourteen. Just a few years ago, he was watching Sesame Street. What did they see in him, those hoodlums, cruising up our driveway blaring their hard rock at us? They had no manners, had a bad influence on Josh, which I was sure had something to do with his mean treatment of Jonathan and his rudeness to me.

One time, I told him that if he couldn't act respectfully, he'd better pack up and move away. And he did. He was gone for three days. When he didn't come back the first night, we called his friends to ask if they'd seen him, drove around for hours looking for him, called the hospitals, and finally, the police. We didn't find him, but later we discovered that wherever he spent his days, his nights were spent in our barn. When Jonathan went out to do the evening chores, he smuggled Josh a dinner of rolls, cookies and Coca Cola. In spite of Josh's bad treatment of him, Jonathan remained loyal. He kept Josh's secrets. He didn't lie to us, he just did not offer information.

And neither did Josh's friends. If they knew that Josh was hiding out because his drug use had gotten him into a jam, they weren't going to expose him to his stupid parents, particularly because doing so would expose them as well.

And we were stupid. We had no idea of the cause of Josh's behavior or how far both cause and behavior went.

That second summer at Sporting Hill Farm, which should have been better than our first one, now that we knew what we were doing in gardens and barnyard and more and more of our friends came to share our tranquillity and beautiful countryside, was for me, tense and anxious. Josh was taking no part in most of the wholesome pursuits of the farm, the tennis, horseback riding, farm chores, and visiting with friends and neighbors — unless he was forced to. He had gotten a dirt bike, a bicycle with wide thickly-grooved tires made to move well through fields and woodlands, and, in the top pasture, he designed and built a series of ramps and jumps with just the right pitch for speed and balance. Paul and I were impressed with his architectural ability. Unfortunately, his new friends arrived with motorized bikes as well, and Josh nagged until his father gave him permission to buy a used one. The quiet serenity of Sporting Hill Farm disappeared.

"The Drakes are complaining about the noise, Paul."

"All right, Pecki, I'll speak to Josh."

But speaking to Josh resulted in the kids going elsewhere, Josh included. They rode their bikes to a trail in the woods that led to a deserted quarry. To get there, they broke the law by riding their bikes on the roads without a license. At the quarry, they were completely free of adult supervision.

One step had led to another. The dirt bikes had been traded in for motorized dirt bikes, and, once the kids had their wheels, there was no stopping them — or their drug use. In other times, they would have been smoking cigarettes. In other times, it would have been firecrackers they were tossing around, not sticks of dynamite.

The constant arguments between me and Josh and Paul about the dirt bike activity, about Josh's long absences from home and his refusal to respond to the family's need for his help and cooperation, made me desperate. Last year, I thought, I never wanted to leave Sporting Hill Farm but now that the opportunity has come to take a week's hike in the White Mountains with my friend Jan, I'm grabbing it. I packed my backpack and set off for New Hampshire, leaving Paul to cope with Josh. Not that he minded. Paul and the boys had a good time together. "Go ahead, enjoy, Pecki," he said.

Jan and I were going to hike the Appalachian Trail. She was my hiking buddy as well as my closest friend and the mother of Jonathan's friend, Matt. Having heard me complain all summer about what was going on at home, she had insisted that she and I go off alone, without any kids.

Our first climb to Mizpah Spring Hut in a beautiful woods of evergreens and birch, 3,800 feet above sea level, was easy and steady and took us through a warm meadow of tall grasses and wildflowers where we ate, rested in the August sun, and I talked myself out.

"What have I done wrong, Jan? It must be my fault. Josh was such a wonderful little boy, so loving and able and responsible. And now look at him. He won't do anything he's asked to do, and he's horrible to everyone but Paul. Sometimes I really hate that kid!"

"I don't blame you. And you shouldn't blame yourself. It's not your fault." Jan's blue eyes were worried. "I wish I could do something to help."

"You did. This climb, this mountain. Thanks for thinking of it."

"Thanks for coming. Shall we go on to the hut?"

We arrived in good time for supper and set off the next morning, after juice and oatmeal, to Mt. Washington and the hut called Lakes of the Clouds. It was a warm day; we were dressed in shorts and light shirts, had our packs on our backs, and were climbing from 3,800 to 6,288 feet by following the two-by-six-inch white blazes painted on trees. When we stopped to eat, we were well above the tree line, and the blazes had been replaced by cairns marking the trail.

"Look," said Jan, pointing at a distant range. "Those are the Green Mountains. That's Vermont."

"Beautiful! Do you know, Jan, my ears have popped open? For the first time in a month my sinuses are clear."

"Guess you're going to have to find a place to live up here, Pecki."

"I don't think I like those signs we've been seeing. You know, 'at this spot in 1955, so and so froze to death.'"

"Not in August, I don't think."

"The weather here's unpredictable, even in August."

"Yes. Well, let's go on to the hut, leave our gear, and climb to the top of Mt. Washington. We can gloat over the fat-asses who come up on the cable car."

We had topped Mt. Monroe at 5385 feet and were feeling strong and jubilant when the wind began to blow. Ahead of us a cloud appeared in the sky, a drizzle coming perhaps. We unpacked our parkas, but, as I struggled with mine in the wind, it was torn in half and blown away. We found that we had to plant our feet in order to stand upright and strain our eyes to see. The cloud had descended on us, the trail had disappeared. Wind was all around us, buffeting, tugging, almost knocking us flat as it shoved us forward head-on into another pair of hikers. The four of us held hands as we were pushed forward along the trail, cairn by cairn, until we were blown against a wall—the side of the Lakes of the Clouds hut.

We tumbled through the door and took a look at the two fifteen-year-old boys we had been clutching for the last half-hour. Sturdy, healthy-looking youngsters with nice smiles, they were as frightened and relieved to have reached safety as we were. "I'm Pecki, and this is Jan." I offered them the hand that they had been clutching. "Were we ever glad to blow into you," said Jan. "So were we," said Scott, the sandy-haired one. "We were really scared."

The boys put their heavy back packs in the corner and started to open them. "We're hungry," Bill, the redhead, said. "We didn't stop for lunch." He pulled out a large boy-made sandwich and offered me half.

"I didn't know I was hungry, but this smells too good," I said, opening my mouth as wide as I could to take a bite.

During the afternoon the winds grew even fiercer and more stranded hikers stumbled into the hut. Pairs of the hut crew went out to look for anyone still on the trail. By evening, the hut was crammed with people, including infants who had been carried in back packs and families who had come up early in the morning on the cable car. Some of the children had no warm clothes with them, so Bill and Scott shared their extra sweaters.

After a communal dinner, we told stories and played cards by flashlight until sleep overtook us. Jan and I were lucky enough to have been assigned cots, but newer arrivals were given tables to sleep on or allotted floor space, as were our boys.

By morning, the winds had died down though we were still under cloud cover. After serving us breakfast, the hut crew advised that climbers not continue along the ridge but make their way down the mountain. They had been notified by radio that the wind-chill factor the night before was thirty-seven degrees below zero, a record for that time of year.

The boys, who were by then our good friends, asked to hike with us. We agreed. Four sounded safer than two, and the descent was slippery. Plus that we were impressed with their courtesy, courage, and honesty, and they were impressed that we had sons their age.

"My mom would never go out on a hike like this," said Bill.

The four of us worked our way down the Ammonoosuc trail to the base road and trees and sunshine. Above us, Mt. Washington was still bonneted in clouds. Encouraged by the sun, the boys decided to make their way to Mt. Jefferson, so we said good-bye.

"What great kids," Jan said.

"Yes, I've got new hope for that generation. I wish all teenagers were like that." Silently, I thanked the universe for putting those boys on my trail.

"They have their good points, but sometimes you've got to get away from them—from everyone, I guess. When our children are grown, we'll walk the Appalachian Trail from Georgia to Maine." Jan threw back her long blonde hair and narrowed her blue eyes in the sun.

"What will we do with our husbands?" I asked.

"They'll meet us every month or so with money and supplies and a hotel room for showers."

"We'll smell so bad they won't want to get near us," I said, and we both laughed.

Chapter 7

Losing Control

Jan was the person I could level with about what was happening at home. Josh was disrespectful. Jan kept pointing this out to me.

"You ought to give that kid a good kick in the pants, Pecki. Where does he get this business of ordering you to drive him around and why do you do it anyway?"

"But if I take him somewhere, at least I know where he is." The real truth was that I would take him just to get rid of him.

"Bullshit! Doesn't he know how to say please?"

There were days when Josh did know how to say please, days when he was his old sweet self, days when he seemed eager to help with the chores — do the dishes, put out the garbage — days when he would throw the ball to me while paying catch with Sixer — days when he seemed to enjoy our dinner-time conversations and even to look forward to the weekend guests.

Then his mood would change. It was almost as if a gear had shifted. He would turn surly, bar the door to his room, and set his music on high.

Even his room had changed character. There were new posters (black was their prevailing color) of sinister-looking rock groups with offensive names like Suicidal Tendency and Black Sabbath.

I detested them and their music but if I asked Josh to

turn it down, he yelled at me. "Shut up! You can't tell me what to do!" If I went as far as forcing my way into his room, we fell into a shouting match, both of us losing control, and I acting in a way that even my worst dreams of myself as a mother hadn't envisioned. I, who had been so critical of badly-behaved children and mothers who let them be so, had become the worst kind of a screamer at the worst kind of badly-behaved child. Who happened to be my own.

Sometimes after prolonged shouting, we were both spent, and Josh would cower like a cornered animal, his brown eyes dazed and frightened. Then I would feel like holding him in my arms, telling him it was all right, that I loved him and wanted to help him if he would only tell me what was wrong. But for some reason reaching him was impossible. He was untouchable, and I was exhausted.

"It's okay, Mom," Jonathan would say sometimes, but I knew he didn't believe it.

At least with him I could talk about the situation. Paul didn't see what happened and I couldn't describe it to him. The specifics of the scenes with Josh seemed inadequate for the reactions we had. "You're overreacting, Pecki, it couldn't be that bad." "Well, ask Jonathan if you don't believe me." I didn't like asking my younger son to stand up for me, but the trust that Paul and I had built over the years was gone.

Tenzing, our large-as-racoon cat was the only bridge between Josh and me. Tenzing loved us equally. Tenzing was enormous — a master cat in control of any dog — and was highly lovable. At least Josh and I could share in his care. He would sit on the kitchen chair next to Josh and wait his turn to lick the milk out of the cereal bowl. I loved watching the scene.

Tenzing was the only thing we could talk about without fighting. His love for us was non-threatening, non-judgmental, unconditional, and when he moved from my lap to Josh's, put his paws on Josh's chest, and licked him under the chin, he took a thread of feeling with him, a strand that with hundreds of others might make a cable. That was at least something.

I told Paul that it seemed obvious that we needed professional help. He agreed, if I would find the person. I found a family counselor, the two of us going alone to see him at first. Dr. Brown quickly saw that we were in disagreement about what was happening with Josh, when Paul called it "nothing serious" and I called it a "crisis."

When the whole family went together for consultation, what we said to Dr. Brown made it look as if Josh was the family scapegoat.

"We have a good time except when Josh is home," said Jonathan.

"Yes," I said, "it's only when he's home that things turn ugly. He even makes fun of us if we laugh together."

"He stays out all night. I'm tired of calling his friends' homes at two a.m. to look for him," said Paul.

And Josh said, "Everybody picks on me all the time."

Dr. Brown's conclusion was that Josh was exhibiting characteristics of the unloved child. (That didn't used to be true, I thought, but maybe it is now. Who could love Josh now, the way he behaves?) He suggested that I show him more trust, let him be a teenager, give him more space.

That, to Dr. Brown, meant not questioning Josh when he came home two hours late from school and not pushing him to complete his chores. I tried, but I couldn't do it. It felt wrong. It was against all that I knew about instilling helpfulness and responsibility.

We went to more than one Dr. Brown in our efforts to help Josh, but without any positive result. It seemed as if the next thing to try was another school where Josh might be happier. He claimed the teachers in his present school didn't like him and he didn't like them. We chose an alternative school, where the students were permitted to select their curriculum and where there was plenty of individual help. Josh went for an interview, was accepted, and agreed to go.

The one drawback to the school was the hour's bus ride each way. Josh had to be waiting outside by 6:45 in the morning and did not get home until 4:30 in the afternoon. But we thought that the relaxed curriculum was what he needed and justified the long bus trip.

For two or three months, the new school went well. Josh was less tense, there were fewer mood swings, he liked the teachers, and was getting his homework done. He began to stay for sports, necessitating rides home in either my or an older student's car, and sometimes arriving home very late without telling me what to expect. But that was a minor worry, major ones were to come later. By the fourth month, his behavior had again become abusive. When I reported this to Paul, who was out of town a good deal, he refused to believe me.

"You're overreacting again," he said. "Give me a good example of this abusive behavior. See, you can't, can you? Ignore him, he'll outgrow this phase."

At that point, I started yelling and, in my mind, cursing Paul for not believing me.

"Don't you trust me, Paul? Don't you think I can see what's going on in front of my eyes and hear what that kid says to me? He's abusive, I tell you." But I was too embarrassed to describe what kind of abuse it was. "What are you doing here, bitch?" Josh would yell at me in front of his friends. "Why don't you go somewhere else? Nobody wants you around here."

Those new friends wore black polo shirts with packs of cigarettes twisted in their sleeves. They wore grubby bandannas tied around their heads. They were rude and scornful to me, wouldn't go home when I asked them to. The new school seemed to be a big mistake.

Not only did I feel that we had made the wrong choice of school, but I felt I was a failure. I had failed as Josh's mother. I had failed as a wife; my marriage was falling apart. I was thinking of leaving Paul. Paul and I had lost our ability to communicate and even our trust in each other. I was becoming more and more unsure of my own worth. Not only was I a failure at almost everything important but I was probably going crazy.

"The way I'm going, Jan," I said to her on the phone one day, "I'll end up as a bag lady."

"With your Saks Fifth Avenue and Bloomingdale bags, Pecki?"

When I laughed I realized how little of that I'd been able to do lately.

"Seriously," I said, "if I should leave Paul how would I support myself? I've been out of the full-time job market for fifteen years. Any job I could get wouldn't pay much more than $8,000 a year."

"You have your experience as educational director of the Nature Center."

"Part-time salary. I was supposed to get paid by the hour, but their budget was so small I never charged them above the minimum."

"And your experience in Nepal with the monkeys. Some women go from volunteer work to well-paid positions."

"Few-and-far-between, I bet."

"Yup. In more ways than one we get screwed."

In the past, it hadn't seemed that way—at least, in my marriage. Paul gave me the space I needed, encouraged my many interests, and never stopped me from traveling. There were times when we didn't always *love* each other, but, at least, we liked each other and could settle most disputes on the long walks we took. Now there was great passion and great pain and little support or understanding.

What held me back from leaving Paul were three things: Jonathan, money, and my determination not to let Josh win. But there was one thing more. Somehow, in spite of Paul's lack of understanding, his denial of what he must have seen going on, the absence of sympathy between us during the day, at night we found comfort in each other's arms.

We went to sleep spoon fashion, holding each other, our knees locked together, Paul's strong arms protectively around me, and in the morning we were still in an embrace. In our warm bed I had the best things of my world: my

husband, my dreams, and the memories of our babies tuck-
ed in with us. And in the morning with his heart beating
steadily against my back, I believed we still loved each other.

Or was it habit? If we loved each other why couldn't he
understand what I was trying to tell him, and, if we didn't,
why was the idea of leaving him so painful?

Chapter 8

The Elephant's Trunk

I was beginning to think that everything in my life was, if not always painful, at least bizarre. Paul's and my relationship seemed peculiar, Josh's behavior crazy, and my interests in dreams and energy fields could be called odd. No doubt they were by my family and friends.

I seemed to be following two paths at the same time — a foot on each — one path, the precipitate descent of the events of my life, the other the slow ascent of my expanding consciousness. It would take me three years to see where these separate paths, with their different inclines, converged and turned into one.

The first path followed the disasters that were happening to Josh and Paul and me. The second was being laid out by my good electricity, my dream life, and my work in the garden. It felt as if I had no choice but to follow both ways, even though I might be split in two in the process.

Marianne Wolf, my friend and dream instructor, gave me a push up the second path. She invited me to meet with a group at her house led by Rusty Carnarius, a red-headed woman, handsome and graceful in pants and tunic, whom I liked immediately, and who teaches a holistic approach to life. (A holistic approach advocates the integration of body, mind, and spirit in both individuals and the universe.) Rusty discussed theories of thinkers as varied as Plato, Maslow, Carl Jung, and Lin Yutang, as well as her experience with psychic material received through mediums. She was able to integrate the thought coming from these diverse sources in such a way that we could see the connections in the different philosophical systems and their possible application to our own lives. It seemed to me that Rusty was a person whose glass of life was always half-full, though others of us might feel that ours were half-empty.

She had been born in China, the daughter of an American diplomat, and had been educated by a Russian governess.

Perhaps it was that unique cultural background that gave her an intense awareness of self and developed her capacity to keep her own perspective. She believed that each of us is responsible for our own lives, our own sickness and health, and is capable of making changes not only in viewpoint but in conduct. At that time, I listened carefully to what she had to say, but I had no idea how to apply her principles to my own life. However, because Rusty had the ability to make each listener feel liked and important, I kept coming to the group meetings.

"You get what you ask for," Rusty told us one day, leaning forward and speaking so earnestly that her silver triagonal pendant swung back and forth.

I didn't ask for Josh's problems, I thought to myself, and then I realized that in a way I had asked for them. I had asked for a child, whatever the problem.

"But you must know exactly what it is you want and are asking for," she said. "One time when I was a college graduate working in Philadelphia, I was almost flat broke. On the way home from work on the trolley, I examined my finances. I had exactly forty-one cents and I needed two more dollars to get through to my next check on Friday. I looked out the window and thought hard about that two dollars, asking the universe for help. When I got off the trolley and was walking back to my apartment house, I stopped to pick up an envelope on the ground. It had no identification on it. I opened it and inside there were two crisp one dollar bills. Just exactly what I needed. If I'd asked for $10.00 — more than I had to have — I have a feeling that I wouldn't have gotten it. If you ask for exactly what you need, you get it. And that will work for you too."

There was a surprised silence, and then several people raised their hands.

"Something like that happened to me," one man said. "I had no money for rent and asked for the rent money — $225 — and got a notice from PSFS saying that I had a twenty-year old savings account that they wanted to close. There was exactly $225 in it. But I didn't realize I was asking the universe for that money."

"I'm looking for a new love interest. Would it do any good to ask for it?" one woman inquired.

"Concentrate on asking for the opportunity," Rusty said. "Then when you meet someone suitable, you can ask the next question, make the next request. You must know the right question to ask."

What was my question, I wondered that evening. What request should I make of the universe? Will you help me save my marriage? How can I save my family? How do I rescue Josh? I sat in the dark in the bedroom and closed my eyes, trying to shut out the sounds of birds still chirping in the ginkgo tree by the window and the irrelevant noises in my head. A question was beginning to surface, a specific need that I had to have answered. I needed to be reassured that I wasn't going crazy. I asked for that reassurance.

The next day I turned on the radio in the car and heard an interview with Phyllis and David York on their ToughLove program. The Yorks were directing questions to their radio audience.

"Have you and your spouse argued about your teen-ager's behavior?"

"Constantly," I said out loud.

"Has your teenager run away overnight?"

"Many times."

"Has your teenager been violent verbally?"

"Yes, yes, yes."

"Has your teenager played hooky from school?"

"And again, yes. . ."

"Has your teenager had trouble with the law?"

Yes. I put him in juvenile detention for stealing Paul's car. Then, I thought of the time a month ago when our boarder's money had been taken from her wallet in her car while she was mucking her horse's stall. She had called the police and accused Josh of the theft. Josh had denied it and later told me that Lynn didn't like him because he had told his friends that she used marijuana. "If that's true, I don't want her here, Josh," I'd said. "I don't want drugs or drug-takers on our property . . . How do you know it was marijuana anyway, Josh?"

"I learned about it in health class. It smells different from cigarettes." He must know—he had gotten his only "A" in that class, I had thought.

I remembered another time when money was stolen and Josh found the empty wallet discarded in the bushes—he said. I blamed the theft on workmen who were repairing the fences. And my silver—forks, knives, spoons, even my grandmother's beautiful chalice—I also suspected the workmen of taking those but I couldn't prove it. Now I began to wonder. Has your teenager had trouble with the law? Well, maybe he should have had a lot more.

"The most important question is, are you satisfied with the way things are?" the Yorks were saying. "If not, the reason is probably drugs or alcohol, and you are already in crisis."

They're talking to me, I thought. They're telling me that I'm not mad!

I heard them give a Doylestown, Pennsylvania, number and tried to remember it. When I reached home, it was gone, so I called information, got the number, and put in a call to the Yorks. Their secretary told me that there were free group meetings in my area, gave me the names of some people to call, and said she would send me a questionnaire. I found out the date of the next meeting and went to it alone. Paul refused to go with me.

The meeting was held on a Wednesday evening in a downstairs room in a local bank building. The people in it, three couples and four singles who seemed to know each other well, made me feel welcome. We were all asked to introduce ourselves and to describe why we thought we were there. Fortunately, I was called on last and had a chance to hear what the others said. One couple talked about their thirteen-year-old daughter who had run away with a twenty-year-old man. "I broke into his room and found her lying on the bed spaced out. It was vile. I took her home, and she's run away again already," said the father, biting at his lips. "Hang tough, Bill," somebody said.

"She needs help but it has to be on your terms."

"He can be picked up for abducting a minor, Bill."

"We'll work on Bill's problem in a few minutes," the leader said. "Let's continue with our introductions."

"I'm Jim Crocket," the next speaker said.

"Our fifteen-year-old son was released from a psychiatric hospital two months ago. He was diagnosed manic-depressive. But his mood swings were caused by uppers, downers, quaaludes, pot, and prescription drugs like Valium."

A woman described how happy she was that her seventeen-year-old son, a twin, had agreed to sign himself into a 28-day drug rehab program.

"How wonderful. You're finally making progress." They seem to care about each other's problems, I thought.

Since my story seemed to be in every one I heard, I was able to describe what had been going on with Josh when my turn came. It was quite plain that drugs were involved. I was not crazy, that much was clear to me. The group helped me understand what had been going on and why I reacted the way I did. I had asked the right question and the universe had answered through ToughLove.

During that period, I was beginning to realize that I had

to save myself first before I could ask for help to save others, and that night I had a peculiar dream. In my dream, *I saw an elephant's trunk—no elephant—trying to open a child's footlocker.* (A trunk, of course. For keeping secrets?) I told the dream to Marianne's dream group, and it was suggested to me that the trunk was searching for something, searching and sniffing. But it seemed obvious that I was getting only a piece of the picture, as in my dream I was seeing only a part of the elephant.

Chapter 9

Jigsaw Puzzle

The pieces appeared as scattered and disconnected as an unassembled jigsaw puzzle cut from a Jackson Pollock painting. Assembling it seemed impossible — there was no sky to hang on to — but assemble it I must. It was my puzzle and I had to put it together.

It was ironic that one of the first steps I took in trying to do so was to send Jonathan to boarding school, ironic because Sporting Hill Farm represented to me the best of all possible settings for a strong family life. That was why we had bought it, this beautiful country property that would be a perfect place for growing boys, and here I was sending Jonathan away. But it had to be done. First, because he wanted to go, and second, because he must be gotten away from Josh who was taking his violence out on his little brother. It was fortunate that we had the resources to do so.

Jonathan and I visited boarding schools and settled on two, both of which accepted him. Paul was proud and pleased about his acceptance, so was I, but I hurt too. I was sending away my support, my smiling second son, who saw the awful scenes with Josh and was still able to say, "It's okay, Mom." But it wasn't okay, of course, not only what was going on between Josh and me wasn't okay but also my using Jonathan as a support system, allowing him to parent me in a role reversal which was not good for either of us.

"Why are you letting him go, Pecki?" my in-laws asked.

"He wants to go. It's a fine school. Paul thinks it's a good idea."

Paul did—but not for the reasons I advanced.

"Sure," he said to me one evening, glaring at me through his rimless glasses, "send Jonathan to boarding school. You've already ruined one kid. I don't want you to have a chance to ruin the other."

I didn't answer, the pain was too sharp, but I decided to do everything I could to be able to leave Paul if I had to.

The second step I needed to take in order to fit some of the tiny twisted puzzle pieces together was to do the best I could for Josh. We found another school, one that was traditional and conservative this time. There was a dress code, a rigid curriculum, regular homework, and an organized sports program in which every boy—there were no girls—had to take part.

But not Josh. He evaded the sports requirement by having a constant sore throat. Actually, he did have a sore throat, and a running nose, as well. He was on medication prescribed for them by an ear, nose, and throat specialist who did not recognize drug-use symptoms when he saw them.

Josh interpreted his success in evading athletics as "beating the system," but, even without participating in sports, his record for the first eight weeks of school was good—a typical pattern for a kid on drugs, to do very well in the beginning of a new program, but I didn't know that then. Paul and I were encouraged by Josh's reports and thought that we'd found the right school for him.

My third attempt at assembling the puzzle had two thrusts. One was to figure out a method of squirreling away money for leaving Paul. The other was to restore my mental and physical health in order to get a job when I did. I needed to be as healthy as possible since I couldn't count on any help from him. I knew that as soon as I left him he would forget me. He had a way of shutting out of his life anything hurtful and unpleasant—and I would be one of these things.

It was Jan who suggested that I sign up for a program

called Health Perspectives, Holistic Approaches to Wellness, which was certified by Rosemont College, a small Catholic women's college.

"To provide an overview of self-awareness, self-respon-sibility, and body/mind/spirit integration," the brochure read. That seemed to relate to what I had been doing with dream interpretation. The course would teach the use of Therapeutic Touch as a tool for sensing and influencing other fields of energy, I read, and that seemed to relate not only to what I had learned at NYU but to my good electricity as well. The course would be held on two evenings a week, and therefore, would be freeing me from the stress of deal-ing with Josh and Paul for those two nights.

I signed up in September, 1982, for the year's course.

The first class was taught by Mary Em McGlone, a Medi-cal Mission Sister, who, to my surprise, was dressed in slacks and a red blouse. Her training included nursing, midwifery, and administration, as well as alternate methods of healing, including Acupressure, Foot Reflexology, Touch For Health and Soma.

The first thing she taught us was Foot Reflexology. She chose a student and demonstrated upon her how to examine and massage the foot with an inching movement of the thumb beginning at the toes.

"Everybody take off your shoes and socks and find a partner," she instructed. "There are reflexes on the foot which correspond to all other areas of the body. By massag-ing them we will be stimulating the body's healing ability. You should begin to feel a sense of relaxation and well-being."

What I began to feel when my partner's thumb moved along my big toe was a floating sensation in my head. There seemed to be a connection between the snap, crackle, pop that I felt in my toe and a lightness in my upper story.

"It's funny, but I hear — no feel — a crackling in my toe," I said.

"That's not unusual. It's a common experience. There

are a lot of theories on what's happening, but no one really knows for sure. You may also feel a lightness in your head."

"I do."

"That area of your foot is correlated with your sinuses."

My partner was now inching her thumb along my little toe.

"Twirl the toe a little," Mary Em instructed. "Make it loose in order to relax the foot." As my partner did so, I felt tension release in my neck and realized that I was enjoying the feeling of being touched and that I had been withdrawing from that experience recently. I had been spending my nights gripping the edge of the bed, not wanting contact or comfort from another body, even Paul's.

As I left the class, I thought of my mother. She had not been well. Maybe I could help her with my new skill. I drove to her apartment knowing that she would be up waiting for the eleven o'clock news, walked in, seated her in my father's recliner (much to his indignation), whipped off her shoes and stockings, and performed lesson one on my mother's feet.

"What a good daughter you are, Pecki. How lucky that Paul gives you so much freedom. I feel a lot better." She looked surprised but very happy that I'd cared enough to work on her, and my father looked jealous. His turn next time, it was rather late.

I'm learning valuable things, even though they appear a bit flaky, I said to myself on the way home, and I remembered what Rusty had told the group. "Don't worry about being flaky; each flake is unique." So at least you're unique, Pecki, old girl, I assured myself.

Besides Reflexology, the Rosemont course included classes on Anatomy, Nutrition, Psychology, and Living Systems, a class taught by the Biology professor. I was astonished that regular professors in a religious institution would teach subjects which could be considered rather far out. The ideas in the course seemed more suitable for a Berkeley than a Rosemont.

The classes I enjoyed most were those taught by Mary Em. They were hands-on classes and appealed to me because I am a tactile person. (Perhaps my mother's constant "don't touch, don't touch", when I was little had something to do with that.) Mary Em was teaching us Touch for Health, which emphasized learning how to become balanced in muscle strength and energy flow.

One day when I arrived in class I had a headache as big the one in the Excedrin ad. My eyelashes felt like great weights and even my hair felt too heavy on my head. The slightest movement made me want to vomit.

"I have this horrible headache. I may have to leave before class is over," I told Mary Em.

"Yes, I see it in your eyes. Your body is tense too. Would you like me to relieve it?"

"Oh, can you?"

"I think so."

She asked her assistant to stand behind me while she stood in front. Just as in Therapeutic Touch, they felt the energy of the headache with their hands and drew it off, down my body, grounding it into the floor. This took about ten minutes while the rest of the class watched.

"The pressure's relieved. I don't believe it. Usually getting over that bad a headache takes two days."

"Do you get a bad headache often?" asked another student.

"About twice a year, usually when the barometer drops."

"This method pulls off pain," Mary Em said, "but it can also speed up an accompanying illness, so you must watch yourself, Pecki. Go to bed when you get home in case you're coming down with something."

Driving through the park on the way home, I was attacked by waves of nausea and the recurring headache. Every time I went up or down a rise in the road, I thought I would vomit. But I managed to get home, stagger to bed, and prop myself up with four pillows since lying flat hurt too much. Because of Mary Em's ability to draw off my headache, I decided to work through it without any painkillers, antihistamines, or other medication. For hours I sat rigid riding the pain, trying to breathe deeply and visualize the headache leaving through a trap door in my head, a technique that Mary Em had taught us. If I moved even the slightest bit, bolts of lightning speared my eyeballs, but even so, eventually I fell asleep. When I woke up the headache was gone and I was rested and alert, quite different than I would have been if I had taken medication. Antihistamines would have left me feeling dry and groggy for a day and a half.

Mary Em had used Therapeutic Touch to get rid of my headache. Now we were learning Touch for Health. We were learning that when a muscle is improved through restoring energy flow in its system, the organ sharing the system is also improved. Touch for Health is built on ancient oriental medicine, chiropractic and standard muscle testing procedures. It's part of a broader field known as Applied Kinesiology.

Driving through the park after class, I sang my own words to the negro spiritual:

The ankle bone's connected to the kid-ney
The wrist bone's connected to the ha-art
The backbone's connected to the blad-der
The arm muscles connected to the lu-ung
Body, nature, God, and universe are one.

What a lot of connectedness. It was making me a bit manic. But how wonderful to know that my anatomy had mind and energy of its own and that my energy was connected to the energy in other living things.

Off to the right, I saw moving bodies and flashes of white. Deer turning back from the road, frightened by my car, probably, as they were about to cross. I slowed down, thanking the universe for its blessing in showing me these beautiful creatures. I felt that they had appeared for me, that the work I was doing on myself had raised my good electricity to a point where it could make connections with the life around me, as well as bring me improved health, even though the well-being I was feeling disappeared the minute I opened my front door.

One of the steps I was taking for the family's health was to change certain things about our diet. Sixer's coat gave me the signal when it greatly improved after I switched to dog food free of additives and preservatives. In the family's case, I eliminated salt and sugar as well. We would use local, raw honey for sweetener (the *local* honey would also introduce pollens into our bodies — help strengthen our immune systems, and relieve our allergies). No sodas, no cakes, no cookies, no potato chips, no candy bars, and no sugared cereals. Although my men complained, I knew it would make a difference in our teeth, blood pressure and nervous systems.

And then one Saturday, Jonathan, who was home for the weekend, Josh, who was in one of his good periods, and Paul offered to help me by doing the marketing. The three shoppers took off. Two hours later they burst into the kitchen and happily unloaded seven giant bags of soda, cookies, candy bars, potato chips, sugared cereals and Tasty Kakes! There on the table were three large boxes of Tasty Kakes. Butterscotch krimpets, my favorite.

"We did the marketing for you, Mom," said Jonathan, a big smile on his face.

I looked at them while my hand started creeping towards those krimpets. All three of them looked thoroughly pleased with themselves. I was about to forgive them when I realized that they had deliberately undermined my effort to provide a healthier diet, one low in sugar and salt. It wasn't as if they didn't know how hard I'd been trying. They knew it and didn't give a darn. It was sabotage, an occasion for seeing red, which I literally did. I was enraged. I took those three boxes of Tasty Kakes, threw them on the floor and jumped and jumped and jumped on them. I saw six staring eyes and three shocked faces as the butterscotch icing squished in all directions. Then I grabbed pocketbook and keys and banged out the door before those open mouths could make a sound.

Chapter 10

Needles

I stayed away the rest of the day, returning at midnight to go straight to my side of the bed.

Jonathan went back to school the next morning. Nothing was said by Josh and Paul about the Tasty Kake episode, nor did I thank any of them for cleaning up the mess. But then, communication between us was at a low ebb. Things were too uncomfortable at home for me to want to be there any more than I had to be. I concentrated on my school program as much as possible, recovering some serenity in my classes, but when I stuck my foot in my front door all my emotional well-being disappeared.

To add to my distress, Sunshine was killed. A distraught passer-by found her run over on the road. We all cried. We all loved her, but particularly Josh. He had played with her, slept with her, taught her tricks. He went into mourning, hung pictures of her in his room and for three days abandoned his mostly-unpleasant friends. I would have felt sorry for him except for what Emma Jean and I discovered.

On one of the searches of the house we now undertook on a regular basis, Emma Jean and I found marijuana seeds in his room. When I showed them to him, he denied that they had anything to do with him, but two days later I found a marijuana pipe, a strainer, and a roach clip hidden in his hi-fi speaker. I took them out and buried them in the garbage can. In their place I left a note: "You thought I wouldn't find

them, didn't you? Mom." And, when I looked in the speaker
the next day, there was a reply: "Fuck off." When I tried to
tell Paul about it, he wouldn't listen. So I called a friend from
ToughLove, "I found drug paraphernalia in my son's room,
but my husband won't believe me."

Our son was getting into real trouble, but Paul thought I
was the troublemaker. No wonder I had a tension headache,
and now, to make things even worse, my ear began to ache.
It was the ear with a history: two breaks in the eardrum and
a blocked eustachian tube. The second break happened five
years before when I was hit in the ear by a racquetball ball.
The ear, nose, and throat specialist patched it and put me on
medication until the drum healed, but five years later it was
still so sensitive that even the change in pressure from climbing stairs could make it ache. To keep it from bothering me,
I had been relying on antibiotics and antihistamines, and
now I wanted none of these. To make sure I wouldn't use
them, I had flushed them down the toilet the morning after I
licked my great sinus headache.

When I mentioned the earache to a classmate at Rosemont, she suggested acupuncture with Dr. Peter Rubin, a
traditional acupuncturist who was a certified internist as
well. On March 3, 1983, I went to his office. I was dressed
like a jock in a lavender sweat suit and Adidas. Dr. Rubin,
tall, thin, dark haired, in an oxford shirt and tie, sat behind
his big desk just like any other professional. I looked around
for pictures of babies he might have delivered with a needle
or so but saw none. Another difference between Dr. Rubin
and most other doctors was that he interviewed me to see if
I was a good candidate for acupuncture before he accepted
me.

He began with some medical questions, and I told him
the history of my eardrum.

"Does your ear hurt today?"

"Yes, when I woke up this morning, it was bonded to the
pillow, and when I lifted my head, the eardrum popped. It
really hurt."

"Does your earache ever go away?"

"Under medication. The only time it got well by itself was when I was climbing Mt. Washington."

"That's a good sign. If it clears up once, it can be cleared up again. What allergies do you have, Mrs. Sherman?"

"The spring and fall types that last about three months. I sneeze, my nose runs, I can't breathe, all that."

"Do you have any other problems?"

"My menstruation has been irregular since I was in high school. Unless I take medication, I go as long as three months without a period."

Dr. Rubin asked about my family history and marital status.

"I'm married. I have two children," I said, and added to myself, one of them hates me, and my husband thinks I'm a liar.

"What is your favorite color, Mrs. Sherman?"

"Orange," I said, surprised.

"And which season do you like best? Which do you like least?"

"Spring, no, fall, no, maybe spring. I hate those ten sticky days in the middle of the summer."

"If you're willing, we'll start treatment now."

The doctor led me to an examining room, told me to strip to the waist, put on a smock with the opening down my back, and wait for him to return. I did as instructed and lay down on the table, trying not to think of the needles that would be coming next. What have I let myself in for, I wondered.

When he came back in the room, Dr. Rubin took my hand in his as if he were about to shake it, told me to relax, and put the fingers of his other hand on my wrist. Then he repeated the process on my other wrist and asked me to sit up.

Much later, he told me that he could detect in my pulses my underlying tension and fear, but he did not mention them because he respected his patients' reserve and felt that their own healing processes would take care of the problem at the proper time. The body has twelve pulses, and an imbalance becomes evident in the pulse long before it manifests itself elsewhere.

"Why did you ask me about my favorite colors and seasons?" I asked him.

"In examining you I need to look at the whole person, body plus mind, or body/mind, as it is referred to in acupuncture. Your attitudes toward your environment are important, as are the color of your skin and any odors you may give out."

"Horror!"

"Sick as compared to healthy odors. Shall we proceed now?"

"I'm ready," I said, though it was a lie.

He showed me a short, thin, stainless steel needle. "This is what the needles look like. They're as fine as a human hair, and you won't feel them. When the needles are in place, I'll be leaving the room, but I'll be checking your progress every so often."

That helped to alleviate my nervousness. I was suffering from a mixture of curiosity and fear that set up prickles on my spine, even though I might not feel those needles going in.

What Dr. Rubin would be doing to me was the beginning process in balancing the body's energy, I discovered later. He was placing the needles on meridians, or pathways, for the circulation of Ch'i energy from one organ to another. For each organ to function correctly, the energy must flow freely in the correct strength and quality. Otherwise illness results. When needles are inserted at acupuncture points on the meridians, they control this energy, either drawing it to the organ or draining or dispersing it, as needed.

He had moved behind me and was inserting needles through my hair into my head, just below the surface of the skin. There was no pain. The needles went in in pairs on each side of the spine, down my back and in each wrist and ankle.

"Sometimes you can see the Ch'i at work, Mrs. Sherman, by vibration in the needle while energy is being regulated. Would you like a blanket while you're sitting here?"

"Yes, please," I thought—thinking it would be something to hang on to.

He put it around the front of me and left the room. I looked at myself. If I were a porcupine, I'd be ready to shoot my quills, they were so erect and quivering. Something was happening to my energy flow evidently. I was feeling a queer sensation around each needle, as if there was a vortex of heat there swirling around its point. I was focusing on that sensation when Dr. Rubin walked back in the room.

"How are you feeling?" he asked.

"Like a porcupine, what else?"

He removed the needles, took my pulses again, and placed more pairs of needles in my head, back, fingertips, and toes. This procedure of removal and replacement continued for an hour until the doctor seemed satisfied.

"How is your earache now?" he asked as he removed the last needles.

"Earache! Why, it's gone."

"Very good. I'd like to see you on Thursday."

When I got home I examined my body. Not a needle mark could I find.

The first six treatments with Dr. Rubin took three weeks, and when they were completed my headache was gone, my sinus trouble seemed to have disappeared, I could breathe through both nostrils for the first time in years, *and* I got my period. The schedule of treatments was to taper off until I would be coming to Dr. Rubin five times a year for prevention and tune-up. This would cost me much less than I had been paying for ordinary medical care, even though my insurance would only pay for part of it.

The spring was now in full flower, and I could go out without a Kleenex. However, although my allergies were cleared, my home life had gotten muddier than ever. Paul was out on business more and more, and I was alone trying to cope with Josh and what seemed like a kind of manic-depressive behavior. The manic part was displayed around his friends: loud music, loud laughter, screeching vehicles, and aggression. The depressive side was for his family. There was nothing about us, his home, or his school that he had a good word for. Most days I had to drag him out of bed and drive him to school since he was too late for the bus.

Sometimes he would be able to tell me the night before about his plans for the next day: a test to take, a report to hand in, but, by morning, he had no memory of the goals he'd set himself, and the dialogue between us consisted of variations on "get up" and "leave me alone."

I hated to begin the day with a fight, and I hated to be obliged to drive a sulky lump of a kid to school, but I had to, unless a neighboring boy named Jerry offered Josh a ride. Jerry was a year older than Josh and went to the same school. He was tall, dark, clean-cut, on the tennis team, and had a soft, polite voice. A decent kid, I thought, not like some of the rowdies Josh had for friends. When Jerry couldn't have a car, I didn't mind driving both boys since Josh's behavior was better when Jerry was around.

One day after school, I went to get Josh at Jerry's house. As I opened the door into their kitchen after a light knock, I heard three shouting voices: Jerry, his mom, and his dad.

"You're lying," the mother was screaming. "Why are you protecting those rotten kids instead of telling us the truth?" She was standing by the stove, unaware that she was spilling a cup of coffee down the front of her soft blue pleated skirt.

"I don't know what you're talking about, Mom."

"Give him a chance to explain, why don't you?" yelled the father, yanking at one end of his bow tie.

All three of them could see me standing in the doorway, but they made no acknowledgement of my presence. Their yelling went right on. Josh was sitting shrunken in a corner as if trying to look invisible.

"Okay then, who burned the clothes hanging on the

clothesline? Just explain that to me."

"I don't know. It wasn't me."

"That's because you're drunk all the time. You're nothing but a bum, a deadbeat. Why can't you be more like Josh? I never smell liquor on his breath." Josh looked down at his feet.

Jerry's mother dragged out a basket of clothes, pulling out one garment after another to show to me. There were cigarette burns all over the coats, suits, and dresses she had hung on the line to air before putting them away for the summer.

"Oh no! Oh, how awful! Do you know anything about this, Josh?" Josh shook his head.

"Unless you're going to tell me who did it, you can get out of this house, you rotten bum," Jerry's mom yelled at him. "I don't want to see your face around here any more. You're nothing but a stinking little bastard."

"Well, whoever did it is sick, pretty darn sick. If I ever catch him, I'll beat the living daylights out of him. In the meantime, Jerry, you make yourself scarce. We don't want you here until you're ready to tell us who did it," said Jerry's father.

Jerry made no motion to get up and leave, the mother and father made no motion to make him. They stood around, paralyzed with rage. I felt I had to do something to break the impasse, to give them all a chance to cool down. Once I was over the shock of seeing what I thought was a solid family break down, I wanted to help them. "Would you like Jerry to spend the night with us?" I asked. The mother was hanging onto the edge of the kitchen table, seemingly unable to stand alone, but she nodded her head. "That might be best," said the father. "I'm going to report this to the police."

On the way home, I asked both boys to tell me if they knew who did the damage. "Whoever did it is very disturbed, very sick, and needs help immediately," I said. There was no answer from the back seat.

"There's to be no drinking and no drugs in my house tonight. You must promise me." They both did.

After dinner, the boys watched television and I wrote letters at the kitchen table. About ten p.m., Jerry walked by the kitchen door towards the bathroom, and I thought I smelled alcohol. "What have you been watching on the TV, Jerry?" I asked in order to get him to talk.

"Some dumb movie, Mrs. Sherman." Jerry's face was flushed, and there was now a strong smell of liquor in the kitchen. Jerry went on to the bathroom, and I went into the television room. Josh was lying on the floor with glazed eyes, staring at the far wall instead of the blaring set. The pile of logs by the fireplace caught my eye. On it was a nearly empty bottle of Jack Daniels.

"You promised, you promised," I screamed at them, brandishing the bottle at Jerry as he walked into the room. Jerry began to cry, and Josh got up from the floor, went to the French doors between the rooms, and smashed his fist through all twelve panes. Splinters of glass flew through the air. Sixer and Tenzing scattered to the far side of the room where Jerry was sitting on the floor, sobbing. I stood there solidified by horror but able to notice that there was not a drop of blood on Josh's fist although there was shattered glass everywhere. I found myself wishing that a sharp piece of glass would slash into his wrist and that he would die.

Later, I went to bed in a sweat suit, my car keys in my pocket.

I dreamed that *I was looking into a deep pond. The water was turquoise and clear enough to see a coral reef at the bottom, with angel and parrot and tiger fish, swimming in and out of the rich marine growth. I was sitting on some rough stones that were formed into a flight of steps. Thick moss covered the banks of the pond, and yellow butterflies hovered over red poppies growing there. The air was drenched with earth and flower scents. This was my own place, a place where I could go or stay as I pleased, a place where I belonged.*

The next thing I knew I was standing beside an arched opening in the hillside. On the other side of it I could see sunlight shining on the pond, but under the arch there was a strip of shadow. To get to the pond, I had to walk through this shadow, and I was afraid to do so.

A lighted candle appeared in my right hand but immediately was blown out. Another candle then appeared. I was able to take two steps under the arch when that light also blew out. I could not continue to walk, through the narrow band of darkness, and out to the sunshine, to the pond, to my special place. I was too frightened. I started shaking all over and woke up.

I realized on waking that the band of darkness was something I was terribly afraid of. My fear would not let me move to the sunshine and serenity of the other side of the arch even though the good spirits of the earth provided me with candles to light my way. I had been shown a place of hope, but I was too panicky, too afraid to go there.

Chapter 11

Soma

When Josh got his driver's license, I was panicky and relieved, both. Relieved that I wouldn't have to drive him around any more, but panicky when I thought of him causing an accident while using drugs. It was the other people I worried about, people that he might involve in a car crash. I'm ashamed to admit that I didn't care if he killed himself. In fact, I spent a lot of time planning his funeral.

It would happen when Paul was out of town. I would pick the simple pine casket of tradition and refuse to put any clothes on Josh under the shroud. Let him be cold in the grave. I would wear a plain black dress, no jewelry — his friends had stolen my jewelry. After the rabbi finished speaking, I would go up to the podium and read a statement on drugs, telling them my child was dead because of drug use and that soon they would be too.

Dead, Josh would be dead — unless I could find some help.

I had stopped going to ToughLove because I was ashamed that Paul wouldn't go with me...but I kept in touch with friends I had met there who frequently invited me back. In February, I started consulting a drug and alcohol counselor one of them had recommended. Paul and Josh agreed to go with me to see her, sometimes singly and sometimes together. I called her after the window-shattering incident.

"He's breaking windows, wrecking everything. He's out

of control. I have no power over him. I have to get him out of the house. I want him declared incorrigible."

"You can't. You have no proof. . .unless there is something in your journal?"

"It was, every rotten thing he's done, it was all there — but he's torn it out. Torn it up — or burned it."

"The only other possibility is. . .you could let him beat you up."

"You're generous with my face, aren't you?" I said, banging down the phone.

I could let him beat me up. So far he hadn't done that. He had struck out at me, come within an inch of my face, but pulled his hand back before he smashed it. Maybe the old mother-child bond prevented him, but how long would it do so? Josh's personality had changed. He was like those black posters in his room of sinister rock groups and a new one of the Grim Reaper, a caped skeleton swinging a long scythe. One day I couldn't stand the vibrations coming from those posters and I tore them off the wall. He didn't hit me then either, but he was furious. And Paul thought that I was wrong to have touched them.

It was Paul who decided to call a highly recommended child psychiatrist. "I'm losing too many days at work chasing this kid around," he told me. We went to the doctor's office, a small museum of African statues, contemporary paintings, and American Indian wall hangings. The doctor himself was tall and fatherly and expensive.

"My fee is $90.00 an hour," he said, "and I will be available whenever you need me. At any time, you can call me and leave a message on the answering machine."

The money isn't important if he can help, Paul's nodding head said to me.

The doctor's calm and pleasant and authoritarian manner gave me the idea that he would be able to take control of our situation. He would be able to do things with Josh that I couldn't.

"When Josh comes to see you, please don't let him drive

home if you think he's been taking drugs," I begged. "I couldn't live if he killed anybody."

"Yes, I understand. I'll set up an appointment with your son, and we'll go from there."

On the way home I could see Paul's relief. He had stopped gripping the steering wheel and jamming on the brakes as if he hoped I would go through the windshield.

"For the first time we're working together to help Josh, Paul," I said.

There was no answer, but his shoulders in his light tan jacket visibly relaxed.

Much later, when Josh was drug-free again, he told me that this respected and respectable doctor, who seemed so strong and supportive, had offered to smoke marijuana with him. The doctor's attitude towards recreational drugs was something we hadn't thought to inquire about.

It was one of the many things I didn't think to question. At that particular time, I was concerned with keeping my head above water, so to speak, in whatever way I could, calling on anyone in either traditional or alternative medical fields that I thought could help me do so. The difference in my approach to the two systems was that in dealing with a doctor I depended upon him to solve my problems — and he accepted that — but in working with non-traditional methods I was learning to depend upon and trust myself.

In April, while we were still consulting the psychiatrist, Mary Em asked if I would be willing to be the patient in a demonstration of Soma at her Center for Human Integration before an audience of about forty people. Since working with my energy was something that seemed to improve my health and also relieve me from some of my worry about Josh, and since I would be learning to work with my energy at a deeper level in this demonstration, I agreed and showed up on the appointed evening.

"The Soma method consists of deep tissue manipulation and exercises which realign the body and recondition the nervous system," Mary Em told the audience. "Pecki will be allowing me to demonstrate on her."

Feeling rather self-conscious in my bathing suit, I lay down on the examining table.

"First I will center myself," said Mary Em, taking a deep breath or two, "and then I will begin what will look like a massage. Actually, I will be sending energy deep into Pecki's muscles and their tissues in order to facilitate the flow of blood and oxygen. In doing so, the muscles will be realigned and the body structure corrected and balanced. Balancing often changes the patient for the better, both physically and psychologically."

That's something, I thought, but will it change the situation with Josh?

"I take before-and-after pictures of my patients. Did you notice that when Pecki was standing beside the table, her shoulders were stooped?" At that, I tried to straighten them, I stretched myself out on the table, remembering that yesterday Jan had told me that I was shrinking. Maybe I am, maybe I am huddling around the emptiness inside of me. My identity has been disappearing, I thought. There's nothing lying here but my shell.

Mary Em had been massaging the area around my shoulders. Now she pushed down on my chest, and I felt hot sharp pain, as if a searing knife was slicing through my body. I could hardly keep myself from crying out, but when she had finished the hour of kneading me from head to toe with that invisible knife, I felt as if I had been rejuvenated, aerated — as indeed I had, since an increased flow of oxygen in muscles and tissues was the result. I felt newly strong and vigorous, the problem with Josh was temporarily pushed out of sight, and I was able to be happy. Even my vision seemed so improved that I was tempted to drive home without my glasses. Before leaving I asked permission to take the other nine sessions of the therapy, hoping that they would give me nine or more hours of healing and serenity. There was nothing like that at home.

At home, I was in the middle of a nightmare. At three or

four a.m., the phone would often ring. When Paul or I answered, there would be silence on the line and then a click. The calls were for Josh from druggy kids who were not differentiating between day and night and who hung up when we answered the phone, but we didn't know that. All we knew was that there was threat coming over the telephone line (real threat, it turned out, because I had been bothering Josh's friends by calling their parents about their behavior). Sometimes, when I was the one to answer the phone, I heard a muffled voice say, "I'm gonna get you."

In the morning, after those nights of threatening calls, we sometimes would find damage—broken fences, blown up mailboxes, trash dumped on the lawn, and, one time, a large boulder in the middle of the drive so that we could not get out.

And the situation between me and Josh was worse than ever. We could not be in the same room without shouting at each other. At four p.m. every day when I knew he was about to walk in the door, the hair at the back of my neck rose. I was terrified that eventually one of us would lose control, one of us would murder the other. Hadn't he threatened to drain the brake fluid out of my car so that I would crash it, and didn't I plan to shoot him in the head in his sleep? Then kill myself, of course. It would be what Paul deserved for not believing me or supporting me, but not Jonathan or my parents or Paul's. They didn't deserve a horror like that . . . besides I had no gun.

I was in bad psychological shape and getting worse. I was isolating myself from my friends, refusing invitations to go anywhere, and, if anyone came to see me, finding reasons to disappear. I had become both warden and prisoner in my own house and was obsessed with my situation. I felt that I had to stay home in the daytime in order to protect everything from Josh and his friends, but, in the evening, when Paul was home, I could at least continue with Mary Em. Those evenings were the only times I was not torn by fright and pain.

At my fourth Soma session, I began to talk about what was happening.

"My son is on drugs, and I'm going crazy, I think. Today I found quaaludes and mushrooms in a shoe box in his room. They're mood changers and hallucinogens. It used to be just marijuana, but now the drugs he takes are worse and worse. I'm so frightened. I can't get help for him. Could you help him, do you think?"

"Well, maybe I could—but first, I think, I should help you . . . You know, the muscles retain the memories of past traumas, physical and emotional. In Soma, we realign the muscles, and that will release tension so that you can make better decisions for yourself, make the necessary changes."

If only I could, I thought, and said aloud, "I'm not sure what you're talking about, Mary Em, but I trust you. And the energy surge I get through Soma seems related to my good electricity. I trust that too."

She was massaging my left thigh when I started to shake, my teeth clattering uncontrollably. The more I tried to stop myself, the more I shook.

Mary Em said she had to get something and left the room. I lay there shuddering. She came back with something in her hand, held it two inches from my chest, and my trembling stopped.

She moved whatever she had in her hand up to my throat and then to my forehead. I began to tremble again. She moved her hand back over my chest, and again the trembling stopped. I began to wonder if she might have a cross in her hand. What would it mean if I, a Jew, had been helped by Jesus?

"What is that in your hand?"

"A crystal." She showed me a long three-inch piece of quartz. "The quartz can absorb excess body energy that is overpowering."

Later, when I told the story to Paul, he said, "It's possible. Quartz was used in early radios to transmit energy, because it will vibrate in response to an electrical current.

It's used to control timing frequencies for watches and in the transmission of data over telephones as well."

Chapter 12

Dubie

Paul understood electronic tuning but not how to tune into our family situation. At this point in our third May at Sporting Hill Farm, we were seeing the psychiatrist, I was taking courses in holist health and Soma treatments, Paul was traveling as much as he could, and the family was approaching breakdown. As far as I could see, there was only one thing that would make me feel better — a puppy.

I perused the want ads and found an advertisement for Puli puppies, small Hungarian sheep dogs used for herding. I chose a black curly furball I could hold in my two hands and named her Dubie, Hebrew for little black bear. I walked into the house with her huddled against my chest, her black furry paws clutching my neck. "With those dark curly mops, you look like mother and daughter," Emma Jean said.

My own opinion at that time was that I was looking and feeling like Medea in her last murdering mad scene when she killed her children. Quite often, I felt like killing Josh. Quite often, I was in enough pain to be insane.

My little black shadow, Dubie, and the Soma treatments with Mary Em helped to give me periods of sanity, periods when I was able to understand some of what was happening to us, when I was able to be in more control of my emotions and better able to cope. Even though abused by Josh and unprotected by Paul, I knew I had to go on with my life, had to make a healthy life for myself. But to do so I would have to get out from under Josh's influence, from Paul's over-protection of him and total denial of our life-threatening situation. I would have to move out of the house and, of course, leave Paul. I decided to go to Jan's. I called Emma Jean and asked her to check things while I was away. Thank God for Emma Jean. I knew how lucky I was to have her help and friendship.

So no one would realize I was leaving home, I took nothing with me but Dubie and my credit cards.

"What are you doing here, Pecki?" Jan asked when I arrived at her door.

"Running away from home is what. Can Dubie and I stay for a couple of days?"

"Sure. We can have a good visit. Sam's out of town, Matt's in school, and today I hate all men anyway. Come on in."

"Right now, I just want to leave Dubie and go to Bloomingdales. I didn't want them to know I was leaving so I didn't bring any clothes."

"But you brought your plastic, didn't you?"

I went to Bloomingdales and bought six pink silk panties, embroidered with rosebuds, and six matching bras; two nightgowns in ivory with ivory lace insets and a matching robe; two pink slips with matching lace ruffles at the hem; one blue petticoat in silk with lace trim; one white petticoat in cotton. I bought four skirts, one soft, beige, gathered cotton with a matching short-sleeved shirt (it would pack well), a white duck button-down-the-front skirt with white bone buttons to be worn with a tan overblouse and a white Aran sweater with bone buttons, a black two-piece cotton and linen suit (in case there was a funeral), a print skirt and blouse in rose and blue. Then, I bought shoes to match all those outfits, low heeled sandals, espadrilles, classic pumps in black and tan, ivory leather scuffs, and new Adidas. I bought black, tan and navy blue belts, Liberty scarfs, one in red print to go with the black outfit, one in blue and green to go with the tan and white. I bought a London Fog trench coat, a Prince warm-up suit in gray with a red stripe, Gloria

Vanderbilt jeans, and three polo shirts in pale yellow, dusty rose, and orange. I charged everything to Paul and made six trips carrying my purchases to the car.

In the drugstore, I bought an Oral B toothbrush, soft; Crest toothpaste; Nivea Cream; Kiss-My-Face soap and a soap container in blue plastic; a Kent comb; Estée Lauder lipstick and mascara; a blue-flowered toilet case; and a fifty cent washcloth. I went back to Bloomingdale's for a three-piece set of soft-sided luggage in black with red trim, including a carry-on bag and medium and large cases on wheels, each with a pullstrap. Then, I went to the supermarket and bought Puppy Chow, two bowls for water and food, and a leash.

When I staggered into Jan's with my first load, she was on the kitchen floor playing with Dubie. "For God's sake, Pecki, did you wipe out Bloomingdale's?"

"No, I left some for tomorrow."

"OK, tell me what's going on."

I bent over and gathered Dubie in my arms while Jan looked at me over the yellow kettle she was filling for tea.

"I'm leaving Paul. Josh was going to pull a knife on me," I said.

"When?"

"The other day when Sara was here. She may have saved my life. And Paul isn't backing me. He told Sara he didn't know what to do about Josh. He's going to wait until one of us is dead before he does anything. Jonathan will be home in two weeks. I can't let him come home the way things are. I have to find someplace he and I can live before then. I think I'll go back to Princeton. Do you think that's a good idea?"

"I think you're falling apart is what I think. Didn't Paul take Josh to the hospital the other night?"

"Yes. Josh asked to go, said he'd taken mushrooms and was out of control. But the hospital told Paul to take him home and let him sleep it off, then call the drug counseling service in the morning. Paul says it was just an excuse so he wouldn't have to take finals. Taking the mushrooms, I mean.

He says Josh has to finish school first."

"First before what?"   .

"Before treatment.' They won't take him anyway unless he signs himself in. No way he'll do that—and we can't do it for him. The law has taken our control of Josh away." I was clutching Dubie so tightly that she was struggling to get out of my arms, so I put her on the floor. The kettle was whistling. Jan took it off the stove and pushed back her hair with one hand.

"How do you mean, taken your control away?"

"In this state, any child over fourteen has the right to refuse treatment unless court ordered."

"Can't your psychiatrist order it?"

"He doesn't think it's necessary. . . But, Jan, I've been getting threats over the telephone from Josh's friends. They say they're going to get me. I've told their parents about them, you see. I've asked the phone company to try to trace the calls, but I'm so frightened when I'm alone that I sleep with my car keys in my hand. And Paul isn't taking it seriously."

"Isn't he worried?"

"Yes, but that's not good enough. He won't do anything to help, and I'm losing my grip on reality, Jan. When the phone was out of order for a couple of days, I thought it was *me*, I thought that the *phone* was all right, but *I* was misdialing."

"Have a cup of tea. You're staying with me until this works out." Jan reached towards me, and I pulled away. Nobody could touch me the way I felt then. Even Jan. If she had tried to hug me, I would have splintered.

Later that evening, I sat in front of the television with Dubie on my lap. Jan and Matt had gone to bed, but I was afraid to go to sleep. The phone rang, Jan answered upstairs and came down to the living room.

"It's Paul. I told him you're here. Do you want to talk to him? He sounds really upset, Pecki."

"No—but I will."

"I'm leaving you, Paul," I said before he could begin talking. "It's not that I don't love you. It's that I can't live in fear."

"I love you too, Pecki. Can't we talk about it?" His voice came over the telephone sounding tired and tense. I felt a little sorry for him, but I had no choice but to get out. "I'm not coming back," I said, "and I'm not talking about it either. Not tonight."

"I'll call you tomorrow then."

When Paul called, I agreed to go out to dinner with him. He took me to Ralph's, my favorite Italian restaurant in the city. While we waited for garlic bread and cioppino at our table in the corner of the dark room, we looked around at the waiters in black and white uniforms, but only sent sidelong glances at each other.

"Tell me again why you won't come home, Pecki?"

"You let Josh evict me is why."

Lines appeared at the corners of his mouth.

"I don't want you to leave me, Pecki. I want you to come home. But, I can't throw Josh out. He's our son."

"How dare you allow Josh to infect our family with his ugliness and his drugs, Paul! If this were a work situation, you wouldn't tolerate an employee behaving like Josh. If it was someone else's kid, you wouldn't sympathize with his parents' weakness. What's the matter with you?"

"Things will be all right. Josh is seeing a psychiatrist, isn't he?"

"They won't be all right. They haven't been all right for the last two years. When we first met, you promised to protect me, but now you don't believe me when I tell you I need protection. You don't believe me or trust me or try to help me—and I'm falling apart."

"I *will* help you, Pecki, you'll see. Just come home." He reached for my hand, but I left it limp upon the table while my insides shrank into a hard ball. That was the effect he'd had on me recently. As Jan had said, when he was near, I shrank—I felt myself shrinking—but when I was alone at

Jan's and caught a glimpse of myself in the mirror, I stood straight and tall. Something I was doing was right for me then. I was able to stand tall and my health was improving. I was going to keep moving up the path that led to those results. I would stay at Jan's, attend my Soma sessions, and *not* go home to Paul.

That weekend, he invited me to a Memorial Day picnic at his parents'. Late tulips were blooming; the leaves on the trees were spring green and nobody knew that I had left Paul. I behaved in an ordinary manner, eating hot dogs and hamburgers, stuffing on potato chips, and drinking Cokes, but I wanted to announce that Paul would not protect me and I was leaving home. "Jonathan and I are moving to Princeton," I wanted to say. Of course, I said nothing, felt my nose getting sunburned and looked for an excuse to go home early. "Jonathan is calling about five," I said. "We have to go."

On the way to Jan's, Paul told me that he'd given Josh two choices, one was a twenty-eight day treatment in a drug rehab, the other was to leave forever.

"Josh says he'll consider the drug rehab. Now will you come home?"

"If you get him out of the house, I might."

That night I dreamt that *I was looking for a key to a house. Finally, I found it and went into the house with some men I seemed to know. I was expecting to have sex with one of them, and I felt very distressed about it. To my relief, I began to menstruate, and the men disappeared.*

In the morning I did stretching and breathing exercises, I thought of the dream, not, however, at all puzzled about its meaning. I didn't want any other man but Paul — that was evident — but I still wasn't going back to him. Not now anyway. I was staying at Jan's. At Jan's, I was able to stretch, instead of shrink, I thought, standing on tiptoe and reaching my arms towards a cobweb on the ceiling. I was able to have a quiet morning routine from exercises to a quick walk with Dubie to fifteen minutes of meditation in my blue-flowered bedroom and, finally, to a breakfast of fruit—usually an orange or apple—and a cup of tea. There was no Josh around to destroy my serenity, and, that day, even Jan, Sam, and Matt were away for the weekend.

About ten o'clock, the phone rang, and Paul burst out at me, "I want you to find a lawyer and have Josh evicted, Pecki!" He sounded as furiously angry and panicky as I used to sound when I called him.

"Why? What's happened, Paul?"

"That damn kid snuck out in the middle of the night last night."

"He's been doing that for how many months now? And you've suddenly decided to have him evicted?"

"If you're taking that attitude, never mind."

"Well, we can't anyway. I've already looked into it, and we have no legal grounds. Not enough evidence of either drugs or thefts. The system works for the kid, not for the parents he's abusing, Paul."

"At least let's have dinner together and talk it over."

At the Chinese restaurant that evening, Paul told me that Josh would not be allowed back in school for the fall term unless he went to summer school and pulled up his grades. "He's agreed to go. He's got himself a summer job in a fast-food restaurant, too."

"So, big deal. He'll still be living at home, won't he?"

"But he'll be very busy—school, job. I'll supervise his chores. Please come home."

"What happened to the drug rehab?"

"He'll do that after summer school."

"After summer school! What do you think he's on—chocolates?"

When Paul took me back to Jan's after dinner, I sat in the darkened living room and wrestled with the problem of going home. I had been living here for eight days now. In two days, Jonathan would be back from school. I didn't want him in the house alone at Josh's mercy. I didn't want him to feel I was copping out either. Thanks to acupuncture and

Soma and their effect on my good electricity, I felt physically healthier than I'd been in years, stronger too, strong enough to protect Jonathan from Josh and his friends. Too, my dream told me that there was no one else for me but Paul, and perhaps at last he might be ready to get involved, might be ready to face the facts of Josh's drug use. I went to the kitchen phone, reached for it, hesitated, pulled my hand back, and twirled the dial irresolutely. Then I lifted the receiver and called Paul to tell him that I would be home tomorrow.

I went upstairs, carefully packed all my new things in my new luggage and put my bags in Jan's attic, caching them away for safekeeping. Who knew when I might have to use them again.

Chapter 13

Back Home

When I drove in the driveway the next afternoon, Sixer and the cats gave me a loud welcome. They were even glad to see Dubie, who was so ecstatic that she ran in circles around Sixer.

Before going into the house, I went out to my gardens. The roses were coming into bloom. There were tremendous yellow buds on Peace, and Fairy was covered with little pink flowers. In the vegetable gardens, the peas were half-way up their trellis. I picked a fat radish to munch and a small head of Bibb lettuce for dinner. Between the flagstones of the walk, wild daisies were thrusting themselves up, and against the white-plastered wall by the kitchen the Dutch Iris made an erect line of blue. Some kind person had filled the bird feeders; I was both happy and apprehensive to be home.

When I opened the door, the house was quiet. Nobody was there, of course. Paul was at work, it was not Emma Jean's day, and Josh was at school. It was nice to be alone in my own house. Through the big window in the kitchen, sunlight made tranquil pools on table and floor. I sat down on the window seat, looked out at the varied green web of the woods, and hummed quietly. Then I went upstairs to change my clothes. As I passed Josh's room, I heard a sobbing noise. Josh was in there crying. I stood outside the door wondering why he was home, why he was crying and what to do about it. Then I knocked. Maybe he wouldn't answer, maybe he would tell me to bug off, but I had to try to find out what was wrong.

"Come in," he said.

He was lying on top of the bed. He turned his head towards the door, and I saw that his face was puffy, his eyes red and swollen, and his nose running.

"I'm glad you came back, Mom."

I started towards him, maybe to take him in my arms, thinking that, *maybe*, he was only a troubled boy after all, but, as I approached the bed, he drew his knees to his chest and turned his face to the wall. "I feel so sick, Mom."

"Do you have a pain? What's the matter, Josh?" I sat down on the edge of his bed, a little tentatively, since he might very well order me off, and laid my hand on his foot, as close to him as I dared to get. I felt no resistance. Could this be a return of the old Josh, the Josh before drugs and hatred got control of him and he turned so ugly?

"I feel rotten. I have a headache, and I can't sleep because of nightmares. They wake me up all the time."

"What kind of nightmares?"

"And my nose bleeds too."

"I'll make an appointment for you to see Dr. Royster."

"No, just let me sleep. That'll make me feel better."

"Would you like a glass of warm milk? It will make you drowsy."

"Okay. Thanks, Mom."

I went out of the room with tears in my eyes. This was the first decent conversation I'd had with Josh in more than a year. (It was also to be the last until he was drug-free.) I went to the kitchen and warmed a cup of milk and honey while a multitude of feelings of hope and sadness wrestled inside of me. When I went back to his room, he seemed to be asleep, so I put the cup on the bedside table and covered him with the orange and yellow afghan I'd made him when he was ten. For the rest of the afternoon there was no sound from Josh's room.

Paul came home at 5:00 p.m., early for him, and I went

outside to meet him. We walked around the property hand in hand, checking the wildflowers in woods and pasture. There were many violets blooming in shades from white to purple. Under the big oak tree, lilies of the valley still made a deep green and white carpet. The pastures were blue with chicory, and purple and white sweet rocket bloomed at the edge of the woods. I buried my face in the fragrance of the bouquet Paul picked me.

"Guess what, Paul, Josh and I had a two-minute pleasant conversation."

"I'm glad you're home, Pecki."

"I wish we hadn't given away all the barn animals. I miss them in the fields," I said.

"With Jonathan away and Josh in the condition he's in, it would have been too much work, wouldn't it?"

"Yes, but I still miss them."

For the next twenty-four hours, we heard nothing from Josh, and, to tell the truth, I didn't miss that. When I opened the door of his room to look at him, he was sound asleep, so I assumed that he was feeling better. Indeed, the next morning he got up for school with no further reference to headaches or nosebleeds. Jonathan was due home the following day. Josh would have another week in regular school and, shortly thereafter, start summer school. I wasn't at all sure how the four of us were going to make out.

It would, of course, depend upon Josh's behavior. There was the barest possibility that the one decent conversation I'd had with him for the last year meant something. The barest possibility that he was trying to change his behavior, trying to break his drug habit, but there was no way for me to be sure of that. (Later on I discovered that any such effort on his part would have been doomed to failure anyway. In June of 1983, Josh was on his way down—into the fourth stage of drug dependency, in which stage drugs no longer brought euphoria and in which he was in a state of constant psychological pain.) It would have been foolish to rely on an improvement in behavior which had been swinging from neurotic to paranoid on a daily basis. I was quite aware of that, so, in order to feel safe when Paul was at work and to protect Jonathan from ugly scenes with Josh, I decided to advance the date for repairs that we'd ordered on the house.

Two bathrooms, dating from the thirties and rotting away, were to be remodeled. Sitting on the toilet in either of them required a balancing act, and showering was a chilly affair since water came out of the pipes in a dribble. With workmen in the house during the day and Paul there at night, Jonathan and I would be relatively safe, even though Josh would be around, since I had agreed to let him postpone the drug rehab program until August. I hoped that with Josh busy with summer school and his part-time job, the three of us continuing with the psychiatrist, and I completing my Soma treatment, the summer program would be beneficial for all.

Upon arriving home, Jonathan reluctantly took up the mowing. The workmen began ripping out bathrooms, and, shortly thereafter, Josh began summer school. Although he was keeping his distance from me, he had toned down his hostility. With Jonathan too, he was getting along fairly well — enough to ask his younger brother to intercept unwelcome phone calls.

Once or twice, I heard Jonathan tell a caller that Josh was not there even though I saw him standing in the same room. I hoped that meant Josh was dropping some of his scary friends. But one afternoon when both of my sons were home, a maroon Mercedes drove into the driveway. From the upper garden, I saw two preppy-looking eighteen year olds (one of whom I recognized as Ned Carter, a smooth, polite fellow I didn't quite trust) get out of the car and go to our front door. Jonathan came to the door, said something, they went in, and in a few minutes came out with Josh. The three of them got in the car and drove off. That little bastard is going off without permission, I said to myself on my way down to the house to ask Jonathan where Josh had gone.

Jonathan was standing on the brick terrace in front of the

door, his face almost as red as the bricks were.

"Those rats pushed by me when I said Josh wasn't here and found him hiding in the living room. He didn't want to see them, Mom, but when they found him, he just went along. Didn't say anything at all. Just went out the door with them, and those guys are *mean*. Josh didn't want to go. That's a kidnapping, isn't it? Let's call the police."

"I've seen one of them before. I know who he is. I'm going to call his parents."

Mrs. Carter said that Ned had gone to the shore with friends for the day. I was angry but I didn't repeat to her what Jonathan had told me, since she wouldn't have believed me anyway. However, when Paul came home, I told him and he was furious.

"Why are you so angry now, Paul," I asked him, "when nothing I've told you before has seemed to get to you?"

"Nobody's going to shove their way into my house and push my kids around."

"Yeah, Dad. They shoved me aside and made Josh go with them. He didn't wanta go, either."

Even so, Josh was gone for two days, and when he came back, he was uglier and surlier than ever. "I had a good time at the shore, so leave me alone," he said to me.

"But you missed summer school and your appointment with your doctor, Josh. That was highly irresponsible."

"I'm allowed a few cuts."

"Okay, tell your father about it. I want nothing to do with your behavior," I said angrily.

On Saturday morning, the Mercedes drove in our driveway again. Josh was still asleep. Jonathan called, "They're here again, Dad." Paul met the two boys at the front door.

"Never come to this house again," he told them. "If you do I'm calling the police."

"We just want to talk to Josh, that's all, Mr. Sherman."

"No. Get off my property."

The boys showed no signs of moving. In fact, Ned Carter took a step forward. For the first time, I saw Paul get ready to hit somebody. Instead he gave tan, dark-haired Ned a good shove.

"You're crazy, Mr. Sherman. You're just crazy. All we want is to talk to Josh." Paul put his hands on the boy's chest again and shoved him backwards off the terrace, towards the car. The other boy backed away, his face twisted into ugly invective, "You asshole, you're crazy, you fucking asshole." Both of them then got into the Mercedes and sped away.

"If I ever see either of them here again, I'll call the police," Paul turned a face red with rage to me where I was standing in the kitchen doorway. He was holding on to his side and breathing heavily.

"Are you all right, Paul?"

"I'm okay, but I'll kill those kids if they come back here."

"You were great, Dad. You sure told them where to get off," Jonathan said.

But every night that weekend we had obscene telephone calls and calls where there was silence on the line and then a click. Paul got even angrier and I got scared.

Chapter 14

The Gift

For the next two weeks while Josh was busy with his job and summer school, the workmen were busy in the house, and Jonathan cut and trimmed the place, I was afraid. I was particularly afraid because I'd overheard the words Josh and cocaine linked by a visiting kid. All that I could do to reassure myself was call Josh's psychiatrist, who told me not to worry about it. Josh was progressing well, he assured me. That, however, did not stop me from worrying since I didn't believe him. There was no evidence of improvement, and I had no one else to turn to for information or possible assurance. If there was a cocaine hot-line to call at that time, I wasn't aware of it.

In order to hold myself together, I worked hard in the gardens and continued my Soma treatments, where, for a little while, I could forget my fears. Not only did I get a break from my fears, but the change in my posture occasioned by the Soma treatments helped to change my attitude on myself. I had more self-confidence and self-respect and was less inclined to blame myself for what was going on at home. My other programs—dream therapy, acupuncture, and Rusty's course in wisdom philosophy—would be starting up after vacation and remained resources for me a phone call away.

One evening, since Paul would be home with the boys, I stayed after Soma for a visualization workshop, in which Mary Em talked us into a meditative state.

"Make yourself comfortable either sitting or lying on the floor," she said quietly. "Now relax your toes, legs, abdomen, chest, shoulders. Breathe deeply and rhythmically. Roll your head from side to side. Now think of yourself as being very quiet, very relaxed. You're in a movie theatre. You're going to watch a film of your own making, and you're the only one to see it. It will be about people who caused you pain when you were a child. You are going to project them on the screen, focus on what they did to you, and then tell them that you forgive them and that you love them."

I pictured that little demon, Bobbie Schwartz, who, because I was a better climber than he was, pushed me off a high brick wall onto a cement pavement, bloodying my knees and making me tear my new sailor dress with its navy and white collar. I forgave him, and I said that I loved him, but I didn't mean it.

Then I forgave short fat light-haired Morris Koerner for embarrassing me by being so very embarrassed himself when I returned the pennies I had stolen from his counter. After I forgave him his embarrassment, I forgave him for leaving the pennies where I could reach them, and then I forgave him for my father for not giving me the punishment Father thought I deserved. Not a harsh word about bad little girls or stealing was said to me. In fact, Morris didn't want to take those pennies back.

After Morris, a myriad of people marched like pilgrims across my movie screen, all of them, whether recognized by me or not, to be forgiven and told they were the recipients of my love.

"Now put your family on the screen," I heard Mary Em say, "your parents, siblings, spouse, and children. Tell them you forgive them and you love them." I had trouble with Paul and Josh.

"Now clear your screen. Look at a field of wildflowers." I saw a Monet landscape of reds, yellows, and blues. "In the distance, you see a speck. It's a person. Bring that person closer, closer, and you'll recognize who it is. It is you. Go towards yourself. Forgive yourself. Hug yourself. Say, I love you." "I love you," I said to myself, feeling more than a little silly, but as soon as the words were out, I felt joy and relief. You see, I hadn't liked myself in a very long time.

My behavior in acting as the warden of Sporting Hill Farm, in snooping after Josh, tattletaling to Paul, being ready to evict Jonathan if the occasion required, and in hiding from my friends and parents, made me hate myself. I had not been able to be my own friend while behaving so destructively. Although I had just finished saying that I loved me, that I forgave myself, I was not going to be able to keep that viewpoint or the relief I felt as long as I had to play the role forced upon me by proximity to Josh. So again I decided I had better get ready to leave Sporting Hill Farm.

In the newspaper, I saw an advertisement for a house to rent in Cape May Point—reasonable and near the bird sanctuary too. Quite remarkable to find a suitable rental so late in the season. I called up, rented it for a month, and told Paul about it that evening when he came home. He was surprised but made no objection. Going to the seashore for a month wasn't the same as running away from home. Jonathan and I would be vacationing alone since Josh had to go to summer school and Paul—even if he could get away from work on short notice—had promised to stay home and watch over Josh. As the cottage had plenty of room, I invited Jan and Jonathan's buddy, Matt, to stay with us for the week of the Fourth of July. I could hardly wait to get there.

Two nights before we were due to leave, I went up to bed early and found myself sobbing against my closet door. Shaking with sobs that seemed to be pushing up from the soles of my feet, pushing against the tangled knot of pain, fear, and anguish lodged in my throat which had been placed there and tightened by what I had been suffering for the last two years. "Help me, help me," I cried out to whatever power might be listening. My cry for help and the sobs coming from my body seemed to dislodge the knot enough so that I could cry freely, without any feeling that I must restrain myself. Released and exhausted, at last, I was able to crawl into bed and fall asleep.

For some reason, the next day Paul did not go to work at his regular time. He hung around the house, at length suggesting to me that we go over those bills requiring payment before I left for Cape May Point. We were in the study with the bills spread on the desk when the phone rang. Paul answered.

"Hello, Ruth," I heard him say. Ruth was the friend whose empty wallet Josh had "found" in our pasture.

"Things are terrible." He listened for a minute or so. "Good idea. I'll look up those numbers and give them a call. Thanks, Ruth. Here's Pecki. I'm going to work now," he said to me, handing me the phone. He picked up his blue cord suit jacket, which was laid on the desk because of the late June heat, and left the room.

"Hello, Ruth," I said.

"I was surprised that Paul answered the phone. What's he doing home?"

"I don't know—waiting for your call perhaps? Somehow he was dawdling around this morning."

"I called to tell you of a successful drug rehabilitation program I've heard about. I gave Paul the information. I've been very worried about Josh since your last letter, and last night I met a young man at Mary's house—her daughter's boyfriend—who had been on hard drugs and is now drug-free. Politest, nicest guy, seemed so straightforward and friendly. He told me that his parents forced him into this program, and that, now he's drug-free, he's back in college. I was impressed with him. He was healthy and rational and looked me straight in the eye. I thought, in fact, that you might like to consider it for Josh. The program's called Straight. There's one in Florida and one in Virginia."

"Thanks, Ruth, I'll look into it and get back in touch. We sure need something—fast."

I called Information, and a helpful operator found the correct number in St. Petersburg, Florida. Whoever answered the phone there said that information would be sent to us immediately and gave me the number of the Virginia program.

That evening, Paul and I went for a walk after dinner. It had gotten a little cooler, and I had on a white cotton sweater because of the evening breeze. The summer sky was still light so I could see Paul's face clearly when he said, "I called Straight today." With the sun down, his glasses did nothing to hide new dark circles under his eyes.

"So did I. They gave me their Virginia number, but there were too many people around here for me to call it," I said.

"I got them. The woman there, a Mrs. Elliot, said that they take kids like Josh. If we bring him down, they'll assess him. I said that I wanted him to finish summer school first, and she asked how he was doing. I said, not very well, and she asked me what I was waiting for then. I told her that I don't really know."

"It's all up to you now, Paul. I'll back you up, but I've tried to help Josh for the last two years, and now Jonathan and I are going to the seashore tomorrow."

I felt sorry for him. His once buoyant step beside me seemed even more burdened, but I couldn't help carry the load anymore. Josh and I hated each other too much for me to be able to help him. Paul would have to bear the responsibility. Josh was up to him.

Jan and Matt and Jonathan and I left the next day. The cottage was not fancy but very comfortable, typical white clapboard, green shutters, and a nice screen porch where we could relax and read or talk, free from mosquitoes. After our swim the next afternoon in water a bit cold because of a land breeze, I walked to the pay phone on the corner to see how Paul was.

"I've told Josh that there are three things he must do as long as he's living with me: summer school, his part-time job, and dinner at home every evening," he said.

"That's fine. I hope it works. How are the animals?"

"They're all fine. How's the house?"

"Nice and airy. We have a screen porch and a quiet beach. We've all rented bikes. Tomorrow, we're riding to Stone Harbor. Hope my legs hold out."

We rode down the ocean road on our way to the Sanctuary to look at a multitude of egrets there. Jonathan and Matt got a mile or so ahead of us, but that was all right with Jan and me. It gave us time to pedal along in a relaxed manner and enjoy the scenery. The day was hot but gorgeous, the ocean dark blue-green.

We had lunch at a dairy bar. I had a chocolate soda with chocolate ice cream, Jan had an orange freeze, and the boys ate hot fudge sundaes, two apiece. We stopped for a swim in Wildwood Crest on the way home to cool our sore butts.

After dinner, I walked to the corner to call Paul.

"Josh neither went to school today nor appeared at the dinner table tonight," was the first thing he said to me.

"Have you called his friends, Paul?"

"A couple of them. No one knew where he was."

The light in the telephone booth was attracting insects, a variety of moths and some large mosquitoes. "I've got to hang up, Paul. There are a billion mosquitoes after me."

"But what shall I do, Pecki?"

"I don't know. He's your problem now, Paul. I did everything I could. I've got to hang up. I'll see you over the weekend."

I had told Paul to bring Josh down for the Fourth of July weekend. There was plenty of room. It would have been mean not to invite Josh, but I wasn't expecting him to bring a friend. The three of them arrived the evening of the third after we had finished dinner. Both boys had on black tee shirts, ornamented with skeleton heads and The Grateful Dead printed above them. Josh and his friend, Phil, put their things in the bedroom and went with Paul to get a pizza. Matt and Jonathan went out on their bikes. While they were all gone, I rummaged in Josh's room. I had to see what substances might have been brought down. Phil had no luggage, not even a toothbrush or a bathing suit. All he had brought with him was the clothes he was wearing and an extra flannel shirt. A flannel shirt for a hot July weekend? I found out why soon enough. Wrapped in the shirt was a pint of Black and White Scotch.

I carried it down to the kitchen, showed it to Jan, and, when the boys walked in, confronted Phil with it. "Is this your whiskey, Phil?"

"No."

"Well, I found it in your flannel shirt and you certainly don't need it." I unscrewed the cap and began to pour it down the drain.

"Wait, Pecki, maybe we should return the liquor to Phil's father," Paul said.

"No way."

Josh had disappeared as soon as I brought out the bottle. By the time the liquor was down the drain, he was back in the kitchen. "Where did you run off to, Josh?" No answer. "Well, get out of here then."

It was three a.m. when Paul and I heard the squeak of the screen door as they returned.

The next day, while Jonathan and Matt were biking or swimming or playing beach volleyball, Josh and Phil sat on the porch steps in their jeans, their Grateful Dead shirts, and dark glasses, complaining about the cottage, the beach, the ocean, the sun, and unexciting, overquiet Cape May Point itself.

By three p.m., Paul apologized to me for bringing them, ordered them into the car, and set off—into a monumental traffic jam, he told me, when I called him at four-thirty the next day.

"I've made an appointment for six-thirty p.m. Monday for us to go to an open meeting at the Virginia Straight," he told me. That meant I had to leave the seashore early Monday morning in order to get home in time to drive to Virginia. I'd have to persuade Jan to stay down with the boys until I got back.

"I've told Josh that you and I are going to a business

dinner in Washington," said Paul.

On Monday, I arrived at Sporting Hill Farm close to noon, and by two o'clock we were on our way to Washington. We arrived on the Virginia side of the city at six p.m., and, in a few minutes, found the building.

We were greeted by Mrs. Elliot, the woman Paul had talked to on the phone. She introduced us to a couple who would be our hosts for the meeting. They looked like upper middle-class professionals, were well dressed and well educated. (In fact, he had a Ph.D. in Engineering, she, an MBA). They took us to a small room, invited us to sit down, and began telling us their story.

"Our son graduated from high school with honors, was on the football team, and was a semi-finalist for a Merit Scholarship. Within three months after starting college, he was taken to the infirmary in a coma," said the father calmly.

"We got an emergency call from the Dean and drove all night to get to the college, to find out that he'd overdosed on PCP," said the mother as casually as if she were speaking about a head cold.

"When we were able to see him, he was in a state of panic. He was sure that he was going to die. He told us that he'd been using hard drugs for four years."

"I'm so sorry," I said.

"Thank you. He's doing all right now. We've all worked hard to make changes. Shall we go to the meeting? It's time."

We went into a large room divided into four sections by four blocks of chairs. We and a dozen other people were shown to some empty seats in the front of one block. On the same side of the room was another block of chairs occupied by parents. Across from us were rows of chairs occupied by boys, and, catty-cornered to where we were sitting — but directly across from the second section for parents — sat twenty rows of girls, ranging in age from early to late teens and twenties. The boys in the front row across from us looked sullen, unkempt, and frightened. Around these boys, stood a number of handsome, healthy-looking, and smiling young men who carried themselves with confidence. It was hard to believe that they had once also been cowering on that front row.

On the beige walls behind the chairs were hung white posters with black printing on them. "Make a searching and fearless moral inventory of myself daily," advised one in large black letters. That meant nothing to me at the time, but later I found out that the slogans were taken from the twelve steps of The Alcoholics Anonymous program, and had been reworded for adolescents.

The room became quiet when a young girl stood up. She had long, blonde, curly hair, a beautiful clear skin with little or no make-up, and was dressed in a fashionable jump-suit.

"My name is Stephanie," she said into a cordless microphone. "Jeffrey and I are going to lead the open meeting tonight." A young man, looking very Ivy-League, stepped up to join her. Jeffrey was the one to address our side of the room. Stephanie confined herself to the side where the girls were sitting.

Jeffrey handed the microphone to a young boy in the front row across from us. "Introduce yourself, Dan."

"My name is Dan. I am fifteen years old. The drugs I've used are: pot, mescaline, hash, prescriptions, uppers, downers, alcohol, PCP, and rush. I've been doing them for three years. I think I'm a druggy."

He was small for his age, very pale, with dark circles under his eyes. He stood there looking frightened and frail.

"Describe an incident from your past, Dan," Jeffrey said.

"When I was thirteen I ran away from home on my bicycle. I'd been suspended from school for selling pot in the john, and I was scared my mom would find out."

A boy that young? Young enough to be riding a bicycle and in so much trouble, in so much pain? I couldn't listen to the rest of his interview for struggling with the tears that wanted to stream down my face. By the time I could listen again, a girl was telling her story. She was seventeen and had prostituted herself for drug money.

"I had to have an abortion, and I couldn't tell my parents about it," she said, staring straight ahead and swallowing tears. I realized that her parents were in the room hearing (perhaps for the first time) about her prostitution and the resulting abortion.

When she sat down, the girls behind her yelled, "Love ya, Missy," and so did some of the parents. They seemed to mean it. I could never say that to Josh and mean it. At that time I thought Josh was evil. I couldn't love somebody evil, even though he was my son.

Then a boy and a girl, seated farther back in the rows of chairs, walked to the front of the groups, took the microphone, and one at a time told their stories. These kids were further along in the program and back in school again. They spoke excitedly about their new accomplishments. "Of course I'm nervous about being back in school, even if it is summer school, but I got an A on my composition last week," said the girl. "I'm really happy to be back studying."

After the boy had spoken of his joy at being able to swim competitively again, an adult staff member spoke about respecting the confidentiality of what went on in the room.

"What's said here and shared here is to remain here."

He handed the microphone to a parent on our side of the room.

"Love you, Son," she said. "Love you, Mom," a young voice answered.

The tears were now running into my mouth and had soaked the collar of my blouse. Paul was holding my hand hard enough to hurt, and his eyes were none too dry either. He wiped them on his handkerchief and passed it to me as a man across the room stood up and said, "I feel angry at all the lies you've told me, Martha. I believed you when you said you didn't take Granny's engagement ring. But you stole it. It was very precious to her, and in her will she had left it to you. Now it's gone forever. You've hurt us all, Martha, even yourself." His voice was shaking, but he added the "Love you" before he sat down.

I wondered again if love was what the parents really felt as one after another they ended their statements with the phrase. By the time the people in the eleventh row were speaking into the microphone, hosts and visitors were given the signal to leave the meeting to take part in a question-and-answer session with kids more advanced in the program.

As we walked out of the room past the two sections of seats for parents, they began to applaud us. If my tears had had any idea of stopping, that changed their mind. I could hardly see where I was going and almost stumbled, in spite of the fact that Paul was supporting me by one arm.

In a small meeting room, we asked the more advanced or upper-phasers, as they are called, questions about their drug initiation and continued use, and then about their experiences in becoming drug-free.

"The hardest thing for me has been going home again and trying to get them to trust me."

"For me, it is the guilt."

"For me it's saying *no* to my druggy friends."

"This program takes a lot of hard work and courage," said the leader. He pointed to one of the girls, a tall thin child with thick black hair. "Sheila can tell you that. She ran away from the program three times and three times came back to start over again." "This time I'm doing it for me," Sheila said.

As the others continued to talk, I put the same questions over and over to myself. How can I get Josh here? Will they take him?

On the way home Paul and I dealt with the first question, to which he already had the answer. He was going to invite Josh to drive him to Washington in the Fiat Spider for a Thursday business meeting. Paul was going to claim fatigue, since he had already driven to Washington once this week and would be obliged to go to Boston over the weekend for my niece Miriam's wedding. He and Josh would spend Wednesday night in a motel on the Virginia side of Washington, check out in the morning, and go directly to the Straight building. Fortunately there is no sign on it that might alert

Josh.

"I'll tell him that the building is air-conditioned and that he can wait in the lobby while the meeting's going on," Paul said.

"Suppose he won't go because of school?"

"I'll tell him I got permission for him. Anyway, you know how he loves to drive the Fiat."

"Do you think he'll suspect anything?"

"No, I'll talk about us flying to Boston for Miriam's wedding. He'll think he's going too."

"That's good. His friends will think he's in Boston."

"You'd better fly down early Thursday morning."

"Yes, he'd never go with you if he thought I was going too."

The next day I drove back to the shore to see Jan and the boys and to give her as much information as I could. "Something is going on, and I can't tell you about it till later. I have to leave here on Wednesday night. Can you stay with the boys for a few days — maybe close the house for me, if necessary? I can't explain. You'll have to trust me, Jan."

"Sure. You know I trust you, dummy."

On Wednesday evening, I called Paul's secretary at her home to be sure that they'd gotten off. "They left at four-thirty," she told me, so at seven-thirty I set off for home. At six-thirty the next morning, I took a limo to the airport, arriving in Washington by nine. A $13 cab ride brought me to Straight by nine twenty-five.

"I'm Mrs. Sherman. My husband and son will be here for an assessment at ten. However, if my son sees me, he'll bolt," I told the three girls at the reception desk. "We'll put you in the side office, Mrs. Sherman. Don't be upset. This is the best gift you can give your son."

It was a long half-hour in the side office, not hearing anything but my banging heart or seeing anything but the creep of the hands of my watch. At ten exactly, I heard Paul's voice introducing Josh to Mrs. Elliot, the woman he'd talked to before.

"I'm glad to meet you, Josh. Why don't you both come in here for a cup of coffee and a donut?" I heard her say, and I heard their steps walking away. I began to cry again, trying to stifle what were shaping into terrible sobs and then to stop them altogether as Mrs. Elliot came into the room to get me. I asked to go to the bathroom first, and, while there, splashed cold water on my face. It was the first of many bathroom trips that day.

When I came out, she took me to the room where Paul was sitting, and began explaining to us what to expect. I don't remember much of what she said and very little of what was told to us by the two women — parents of children in the program — who stayed with us the entire day in order to give us support. If I close my eyes, I can see one face only, that of a middle-aged blonde, who for some reason seemed to me to be rather happy-go-lucky. It wasn't that I was disinterested or ungrateful for the women's support, it was that all of my senses were numb. However, without being aware of what I was saying or doing, I gave the right answers, evidently signed my name where Paul designated, managed not to go on crying, and listened to the stories of the "intake parents" without really hearing them. I was in a state of shock, but at a certain level I responded. At a certain level, I knew we were in the right place and were doing the right thing for Josh.

After about an hour, Mrs. Elliot came into the room holding a pouch of marijuana, a pipe, a roach clip, and a few pills. "These were in Josh's clothing." I listened closely then.

"What? I spent the night with him. I was sure he was clean," Paul said.

"Your son has admitted to using cocaine, pot, alcohol, hash, hash oil, LSD, mushrooms, ludes, nitrous oxide, rush, and Thai stick. He doesn't think he needs the program, though." She threw out her hands in a shrug. "Mr. Sherman, do you want to talk to him? I believe that it's time for the assessment to become an intervention."

"What's an intervention?" I found myself concentrating on her answer.

"In an intervention, upper-phasers, as well as staff members — all of them recovered drug users — will talk with Josh, tell him their stories, and confront his evasions. Sometimes it takes fifteen minutes and sometimes a whole day. Peer pressure got him into trouble, Mrs. Sherman, and peer pressure will get him out."

Paul followed her out of the room in a no-nonsense manner but was back in ten minutes looking chagrined. For the next few hours, we sat on our chairs around a big desk in the little room doing a great deal of fidgeting. Paul drummed his fingers and I made bathroom trips between assurances from the intake parents that Josh would agree to stay.

But neither Paul nor I were sure. At any moment, we thought he might burst through the door, run at me, cursing, and then out of the building, not to be seen again.

"Don't worry, we've had experiences with these kids. We expect them to get panicky and want to run, but we can deal with that," Happy-go-lucky said. "How did you manage to get him here?"

"He drove me down. He loves to drive my sports car. He was worried about missing summer school, but I told him that he had permission to come. I got a scare at the motel last night, though. Josh was flipping the dials, and he flipped onto a program about adolescent drug abuse. Straight was mentioned. I had a hard time not asking him to change the station, but he lost interest and switched to something else."

"That was a close call, Paul."

"It seems as if a higher power intervenes sometimes," said Mrs. Happy.

If so, it took its time. It was 5 p.m. before Josh agreed to stay. Although we could have signed him in, the administration wanted him to do it himself as a first step in becoming responsible for his own actions.

Somehow we got through the long day, but, looking back on it, I don't know how. There are only parts of it that I can remember. We must have done a lot of talking, eaten lunch, I must have made twenty or more bathroom trips, but all that remains a blur.

When Josh had finally signed himself in, we were told that we could see him to say goodbye. He was slumped in a chair, his arms hanging, his face streaked with tears. I could see the defeat in his eyes. Maybe for the first time, I thought, Josh has had to look at himself. Seeing him so spent and defenseless, I was overwhelmed with love for him, but he didn't look at me. He looked only at Paul and said, "You're nothing but an asshole too."

"I love you, Josh," Paul said, "and we're going to help you save your life."

Yes, we're giving him the gift of his life, I thought, remembering what the girls at the desk had said to me in the morning.

As we left, Mrs. Elliot reminded us to come to the open meeting the next night. She took us each by the hand and said, "Go home and heal yourselves."

Anxious as we were to do so, it was rush hour in Washington, so we pulled into a Howard Johnson for dinner. Our carrot-red-dyed-haired waitress greeted us with a wide smile and, "Did you-all have yourselves a ni-ice day?"

"Yes, we had a wonderful day," I said.

When she left with our order, Paul and I collapsed on the table and laughed and cried and laughed.

Chapter 15

Wedding Dance

It was the last laughing but not the last talking of the day.

On the way home, Paul told me that earlier in the week he had consulted Dr. Brown about putting Josh in a long-term drug rehabilitation program, and that the psychiatrist had said, "It's premature and too dramatic, Mr. Sherman."

"Too dramatic! If he wants to hear something dramatic I'll read him the list of Josh's drugs," I said.

We stopped talking. We were both exhausted, and the Beltway was demanding Paul's concentration. I slumped down in my seat, trying not to see the picture of Josh slumped in his chair with a defeat in his eyes which I couldn't seem to forget.

"It will be two years before this is over, Pecki," Paul said, as if he'd just been given the information. If that's true, it will be another two years for me to have a chance to grow, I thought, knowing how hard that was going to be but also that I would have to do it. If there is such a thing as more than one life, I don't want to repeat this one.

The very next afternoon we were back on 95 on the way to another meeting. We made it through the construction in the Baltimore tunnel by 4 p.m., which meant that we would arrive on time. We were beginning a pattern that we would be following for the next year: rushing to Washington at least once a week in the late afternoon, missing our dinner, receiving four or five hours of emotional battery, and at midnight driving three hours home again to arrive there too stimulated and exhausted to sleep.

We arrived exhausted as well at the first meeting, too exhausted to say anything or even acknowledge the presence of Josh, who sat across from us in the boy's group, slouched so far down in his seat that we could only see the top of his head, which was enough, however, to notice that somebody had cut his hair. "Well, he's still here anyway," I said to Paul.

On the way home after the meeting, in order to keep us awake, Paul put on the tape of the Soviet Army Chorus. They were singing, "It's a long, long way to Tipperary," and somehow they reminded Paul of a long ago conversation.

"It must have been eighteen years ago," he said," because we didn't have Josh yet."

"What conversation?"

"With Allen Maller. He said that we would recognize the Messianic age when it arrived because at that time sons and fathers would be able to talk together. . . I totally rejected the idea. At that time I thought that fathers and sons talking together was what happened all the time. But Josh and I don't talk. Haven't talked for years, have we? I didn't realize that till tonight."

"You and I and Allen used to talk till one a.m. (That's what it is now by the way.) The night the priest was there, they went on talking, and you and I fell asleep. We leaned on each other like empty bookends. . . I really wanted to hear that conversation too."

"So did I. Allen knows a lot about doctrine, even Catholic doctrine."

"What do you think he'd think of us now that we're in all this trouble, Paul?"

"He'd find some good in it somewhere."

"*Oh, no John, no John, no-o, John, no*," sang the Soviets.

"I told Esther I'd be a damper at the wedding, but she said, come anyway, she's used to me. What do you think?"

"Let's go."

We left for the wedding Saturday morning, flying to Boston with Jonathan whom Jan had brought home on Friday after finding a sub-rental for the Cape May house for me. On the flight, we undertook the job of telling Jonathan where Josh was. "So that's where you were. I'm glad he's getting help." Jonathan nodded his dark head. You're in it too, my boy, I thought to myself. You'll find out soon enough. "Don't talk this over with anyone but family," I said aloud. "Josh's friends are not to find out about it yet. They think he's in Boston too. We don't want to give the teenage Mafia anything to work on. They might try to spring Josh if they knew where he was."

The plane was beginning its descent to Logan at that moment, and the stewardess reached in front of me for Jonathan's coke glass.

We rented a car at the airport, drove to our hotel and got dressed for the wedding. I had on a simple turquoise silk, very becoming to my tan. Paul wore a pale blue linen jacket and navy slacks, Jonathan a navy blazer and white slacks. The Hupa was already up when we took our seats in the small room of the suite in our hotel where the wedding and reception were to be held. Two of my nephews were amongst the four men holding up the wooden poles which supported the canopy decorated with daisies, white roses and stephanotis. Their fragrance flooded the room.

There was a little stir behind us when we took our seats in the third row. People whispering, and across the aisle Aunt Fanny giving me significant looks. In a few seconds she heaved herself out of her seat, said hello to Paul, and to me, "Esther told us about Josh. It's a good thing, Pecki. I'm glad you're here," and went back to her place. A hand on my shoulder was my mother saying hello. In a long softly-colored flowered dress, she sat down in the row ahead of us. My father looked distinguished in a gray suit and a paisley tie, something that as a Zionist he didn't ordinarily wear.

The Mendelssohn wedding march had begun. Miriam, the bride, walked down the aisle looking beautiful in white lace, a wreath of stephanotis holding her tulle veil. (In

Greek, stephanotis means flowers suitable for a wreath, I remembered from looking up the spelling in a dictionary.) There was stephanotis as well as white orchids in her bouquet.

After the ceremony, there was dancing in the larger room of the suite to the music of a Klezmer band, which played a blend of Eastern European folk and dance music and American jazz. Wonderful Yiddish music that brought out the gypsy in me. Somehow the music of the clarinet managed to put all of the trouble of the last two years out of my consciousness, and I danced and danced and danced. I danced with Paul, with my mother, my sister, the bride, Aunt Fanny, Uncle Sam, other strange gentlemen, and by myself. While I was dancing with one partner, his wife advanced, cut in, and took him away. I went on dancing alone.

"I wish I could be as carefree as you are, Pecki," said Evelyn, my sister's friend. Carefree I was certainly not! "A wedding dance to Klezmer music should uninhibit anyone," I said, and thought that, if she'd seen me yesterday, she'd know my dancing was only a testimony to the band. The music had popped my cork.

Chapter 16

Open Meeting

At Straight the next Monday night, we were astounded to see Josh sitting bolt upright on a seat in the first row of the boys' section.

"That means he's supposed to speak tonight," Paul said.

"I can't believe that he really will," I said, wanting to hide under my chair, whether he did or not. Sweat was pouring out of my glands so freely that I looked at the woman next to me to see if she were covering her nose against its acrid odor. If Josh refused to talk, what would I do? On the other hand, if he did talk, what would he say and what would I do when he said it? When the microphone came to me, what would I find to say in response to whatever he had said previously? We were instructed to talk about feelings only. No recriminations or moralizing. "I feel . . . about . . . because . . ." was the formula, but I was ready to lecture. My feelings were much too raw to want to talk about them.

Josh was the second boy to be handed the microphone. He stood up—all six feet of him—and began in a shaking voice that he tried to make sound tough, "My name is Josh. I am sixteen. I've been doing drugs for four years. The drugs I've done are: cocaine, pot, alcohol, hash, hash oil, LSD, mushrooms, ludes, nitrous oxide, rush and Thai stick. Now I have to tell a story about my past. I was with a bunch of my druggy friends when we decided to form a club. Our initiation was to burn ourselves with a joint. I was scared, but I was out of it too, and I didn't feel myself burning my arm until the next day. I told my parents that I'd burned myself working on a car. I still have the scars." (More than a year later, Josh told me that he was glad that he had those scars to remind him of what he'd done and not ever to do anything like that again.)

Josh was continuing: "I stole my mother's silver, sold it for money to pay off my supplier. The night I stole the silver, I was afraid to go home, but they didn't even suspect me."

At that point, I guess my ears blanked out (if such a thing is possible) since I heard nothing further that Josh had to say. Paul said that he talked for a few minutes about his short-term goal which was to memorize the seven steps of the program.

For the next hour, I sat in the room hearing parts of incredible story after incredible story, drenched in my acrid sweat and battered by breakers of emotion. Then the microphone came to me. I got to my feet determined to look strong, speak out, and not cry, but all that I was able to do was mumble that I was glad Josh was safe and alive and that the rest of us were too.

In his turn, Paul said that he was going to do his best to rebuild the family. He then passed the mike to the woman next to him who began, "I'm so disappointed," when she was interrupted by a boy in the fourth row who stood up and yelled, "Coming home, Mom," and ran to hug her. It seemed to me that the whole room rocked. It's a room where despair and hope sit on the same row, I said to myself, as I looked at Paul beside me with tears streaming down his face.

The next day I started calling the parents of Josh's druggy friends.

"This is Pecki Sherman, Josh's mother. I'd like to have a talk with you about what's been happening with Josh. Could you give me a few moments as soon as you can?" Most of them agreed to see me.

My intention was to expose to them what Josh had been doing and to warn them of the likelihood that their children were doing the same thing. They were polite enough to thank me but so deeply in denial that they were not about to take any steps to deal with their children's problems. I wondered if my efforts had any result at all except to confirm their opinion of me as a troublemaker.

Then I called Dr. Brown and read him the list of eleven drugs that Josh had admitted taking. "It's those eleven substances that have caused the problems in our family. We've been exhibiting the symptoms of people connected to someone with a chemical dependency, I've discovered. Our pattern was classic. How could you have escaped knowing about it, Dr. Brown? If you'd looked into it, you'd have found out that drugs were responsible for Josh's behavior. And he isn't the only one either. You have two other patients who've been using drugs with him." I felt that Dr. Brown knew who they were.

I got a lot of pleasure out of shaking him up, but I didn't stop there. I went to see the police chief, told him Josh's history and that he wasn't alone in our neighborhood in abusing drugs, that there were many other kids there who did. From the look of relief on his face, I gathered that he thought our local crime wave was over now that Josh was out of the state. He wished me a lot of luck and beamed me towards the door.

In spite of my efforts, the police chief did not round up either suppliers or users, the druggy kids were still spaced out, and Dr. Brown made no statement about drugs being the root of his patients' problems. It seemed as if I had made no difference in the attitude of parents, police, or the psychiatric profession. Nobody wanted to hear what I had to say, and, two weeks later, the crime wave resumed. Six houses were broken into and robbed.

Still, even though I'd had no success in spreading my information in my immediate neighborhood, I knew that there were desperate people out there that I could help. Barbara and Rich Deaver were two of them. I had met them in ToughLove and had heard that in spite of all they had tried to do their seventeen year old son had been out of control for several years. When I spoke to Barbara about Straight, she said that she'd like to hear more about the program from Paul and me. Previously, Paul had assumed that anyone with a problem kid was a problem parent, but meeting the Deavers at a party one night had persuaded him that he was wrong. "Rich Deaver's a good analytical thinker," Paul had said, "and Barbara seems very steady."

When they arrived at our house the evening after my phone call, Rich Deaver got right to the point, while he was still standing in the center of our living room. "Andy will be eighteen in three months and able to leave home. If we're going to help him, we have to act immediately." He began to pace nervously while Barbara talked.

"We've done everything in our power to try to straighten him out, but nothing's helped. Tell us everything you can about the program."

Rich furled his six-foot frame on our sofa and leaned forward to listen while Paul, a bit tensely, talked.

"Well, it's tough. It's like—the Marines."

"I know what you mean. I was Navy, but either way it's boot camp."

"I mean, it's really tough," Paul repeated. "New kids in the program are never allowed to be alone. Someone holds them by a belt loop at all times during the day—that's so that they won't bolt—and at night, they're locked into their bedrooms."

"Where, at Straight?"

"No, in the home of a host family whose kid is more advanced in The Program. That's where Josh is, but we don't know who they are." He brushed his hair back from his forehead and looked at me. I laughed nervously.

"But what happens when they go to the bathroom?" Barbara asked, her blue eyes looking shocked.

"Someone goes with them."

"They can't be trusted yet, you see," I said, suddenly feeling that I would wet my pants if I didn't go soon myself.

"They have to earn the privilege of going into the bathroom alone."

"Some privilege!" Barbara seemed outraged.

"Excuse me," I said, leaving.

"I know it sounds severe, but that's the only thing that works. The kids can't be trusted because their mental processes are drug-distorted," Paul was saying as I went out into the hall. "So they have to see it for themselves," Rich was saying when a few moments later I came back into the room.

Paul was making a tent with his hands, touching the fingertips and then the palms together, in the way he does when he's thinking hard. Centering himself, I suddenly understood.

"They become panicky. They're so used to depending on mood-altering substances that when they're taken off them, they get out of control. The structure then provides a certain security, you see."

"You see, we've become three-week experts, Rich," I said, laughing my nervous laugh. "Would you like some iced tea or would you prefer a Coke?"

"Iced tea would be lovely. Oh, are these raspberries from your garden?"

"I picked them today at the edge of the woods . . . . The program uses the twelve AA steps, redesigned for the adolescent."

"What really makes it work is that the kids take responsibility for each other. Peer pressure is what got them into trouble and peer pressure gets them out," Paul said.

"What do you really think of the program, Paul?" Rich asked, concentrating his eyes on Paul's face.

"It's a real bitch. It's time-consuming, heart-breaking, shocking. But there are parents there who are giving their lives to helping kids — their kids and ours — and it looks as if it works."

"How much does it cost?" asked Rich.

"The complete cost is $4,000.00 — no matter how long it takes the kid to complete the program — and after care treatment's included."

Barbara and Rich exchanged glances. "Okay, we'll go with it. We've paid more than $7,000.00 to the psychiatrist in the last year. And since the program's out of state, we can force him to go there. If we don't, in three months, he'll be eighteen, and we'll lose all control of him," said Rich.

A week later, I got a call from Barbara saying that Andy Deaver was in Straight. For the next six months, or 18,000 miles, we drove back and forth to Virginia with the Deavers, except for the trip we made with fourteen-year-old Jonathan when it was time for him to speak to Josh on the microphone.

"I don't have anything to say to him. What am I supposed to say?"

"Tell him how you feel. You can say whatever you want about the way you feel, but he won't be able to respond to you. He hasn't earned that right yet."

"You mean he can't talk to me!"

"Talking to his family is considered a privilege. He can't receive that privilege until his fourteenth day in the program."

"Why do I have to go see him at all? I won't be here this fall. I'll be away at school."

"The whole family has to be involved. It's a family program. We all have to learn from it. The education won't hurt you. Amongst other things, we've been learning that chemical dependency is a disease."

"Well, I don't have a disease."

"That's true. You're not chemically dependent. Dad and I aren't either, but we are co-dependents because we have not been functioning rationally. Our family has reacted in unhealthy ways to Josh's dependency."

"What ways?"

"Dad denied that there was any problem. He didn't want to hear about it. That wasn't healthy. And I behaved hysterically. You probably remember that."

"You sure yelled a lot all right."

"And your own reaction to Josh's behavior had its good and bad sides."

"Yeah, I helped him to run away, didn't I?"

"Well, that wasn't so bad. You were being loyal even if that wasn't helping him. What happened in our family was that we tolerated disruptive behavior. When Josh broke rules, we didn't know how to discipline him, so we disregarded the old rules and made new ones. That wasn't a healthy attitude. The more out of control Josh got, the more irrational were our responses to him. We didn't know that he was uncontrollable because of drugs, and that nothing short of eliminating the drug would turn him into a healthy human being. That's what we're all learning now and that's why you have to be involved."

"I still don't see what it has to do with me."

"It's the way it is, that's all. We need your help, Jonathan."

"Okay, but I don't like it."

We sat in the back row this time, Jonathan between us for our and his reinforcement. The microphone, moving back and forth along the row, reached Paul first. We all three stood up.

"I'm really glad that we found the program, that you're getting help, Josh, and that I'm beginning to understand the reasons for my denial," said Paul. "You see, I was brought up never to admit that anything about me or my family or my life could be wrong, and so I couldn't admit your drug problem. I love you, Josh."

He handed the microphone to Jonathan, who took it like a hot poker, straightened his shoulders, began. "I'm gla-a," doubled over as if he had been kicked in the stomach, and broke into loud sobs. Paul and I placed our arms around him, I picked up the mike, held it for a few seconds unable, unwilling to speak. Under my compassion for Jonathan was rage at Josh for making us all suffer so.

"No one," I burst out, "has called me 'whore' or 'asshole' for the last ten days, and I'm beginning to believe I never was one." I passed the microphone on without the customary "love you," but even through my tumult, I heard Josh say pleadingly, "Love you, Dad. Love you, Jonathan. Love you, Mom."

"I'll never go back there again," Jonathan said on the way home.

However, he did. For the rest of the summer he occasionally traveled back and forth with us and the Deavers to take part in the sibling program. The rest of the time he went on with his summer life, working on the farm, bike riding with Matt, and occasionally weekending at the shore with boarding school friends. He seemed to be able to put Straight out of his mind.

Chapter 17

Black Cloud

Paul and I were not so lucky. We were attending meetings once a week (I, often twice), were absorbed with what was going on in The Program between times, and were trying to do what we could to heal ourselves. We both had to work at it. It was apparent to me that the studies I'd been undertaking were part of that work and that there was a synchronicity (at least, in my opinion) in the way I had discovered the alternate health methods that I'd found so helpful. When my foot had needed a step to climb on, the step had presented itself — whether it was dream interpretation or Soma or Straight. When you look for help, you find it, and that's synchronicity.

Certain things about my ordinary life were helpful to my healing too: hard work in the garden, for instance, and cooking the fresh food which was its result. Anything creative helped my good electricity, and that helped me continue to make changes physically, psychologically, and emotionally.

I called Mary Em to tell her about it.

"We've gotten Josh into a long-term drug rehabilitation program."

"Good for you! You've made big changes in your life, haven't you? You found the courage to refuse to take all the responsibility for what was going on at home. That was a big change."

"The Soma treatments helped me. That hot knife of

yours . . ."

"Yes, it was obviously something you needed. However, your experience of physical pain is quite different from most people's experience with Soma."

"It took that pain to crack my shell. Otherwise, I would have blocked the treatments. Prevented them from getting inside, somehow. But your searing knife wouldn't let me do that."

"Don't give me all the credit, Pecki. It was you who chose to take the treatment and you who are making the changes, you who stood, excuse the expression, straight. Holistically speaking, you did very well. Body, mind, spirit — and wardrobe!" We both laughed.

As the summer wore on, Josh was changing too. He had earned "talk", as they called it, on a regular basis, and, for the first time he was telling us the truth about his drug life. How he had used beer and marijuana with his older cousin and how he himself had sold drugs to his friends, for instance. This is when we learned that his arm had been broken by two inmates of the juvenile detention facility. That was quite a shock to me. Obviously, Josh's broken arm was a result of my overreaction, Paul's and my lack of communication, and our total misunderstanding of Josh's involvement with drugs. The knowledge made me ill.

As did his description of his druggy days as well: how some mornings he woke up in strange places, not knowing where he was, how he got there, or what drugs he had taken the night before. And how many times he was convinced that someone was trailing him, spying on him. "That was me, Josh," I said.

"No, I knew when you were doing it. This was different. There were shadows following me. If I looked in the mirror, I saw them behind me, but, if I turned around they were gone. If I looked in the mirror again, where my face should have been was a death's head, a skull. I was scared all the time." Tears were running down his cheeks.

"You looked threatening to me, not scared. I was the one

who was scared all the time. You were so ugly, and you never told me the truth. How could you have told all those lies?"

"The first one was the hard one. After that it was easy. Once I started lying there was no way to stop." He raised his arm to wipe the end of his nose on his sleeve, and I handed him a tissue. We were talking in a small room, had been talking for some minutes, and I was feeling sorry for him but proud that he was able to tell me the truth about himself. It had been very hard for him to do so, although, little by little over the weeks, his attitude had been changing, even if in degrees as small as the seconds on the face of a clock. I could almost hear the clicks as Josh moved forward. I felt my clock moving with his. We were both softening, broadening, deepening. We were both growing, but both had a long way to go. On our clock faces, there were 3540 seconds ahead.

Not only were Josh and I working with our clocks, but others in the program were busy with their own time frames. Some kids were advancing, some dropping back or out, and some graduating. I admired these particularly. They were so clear-eyed, healthy, and handsome. Even they were a little bit scared, perhaps, but moving ahead and optimistic about their eventual success.

Paul had been making changes too. However, even though he was now involved in Josh's recovery and in talking to the parents of other druggy kids, even though I understood more about his previous denial, I was not at that time able to forgive him. What in me had been overwhelming fear had turned to consuming anger. I was furious at Paul for what he had put me through. I'm ashamed to admit that I took almost every opportunity to remind him of his blindness and lack of trust in me.

"Do you remember last year when Josh smashed the windows and you said it must have been my fault? I must have done something to provoke him, nagged him probably until he lost control? And all the time it was the cocaine he had been taking. Do you remember that, Paul? You never even told me you were sorry, did you?"

"I am sorry, Pecki. You know that. What do you want me to do, grovel?"

"Yes, so I can stamp on you. Hobnail boots too. That's what you deserve."

"Hobnail boots? You really hate me that much?"

"I do. I really do."

"Well, I'm not getting down on my knees to you, if that's what you want."

"I do want. In front of other people too. My parents, your parents, Jonathan, Sara."

"Enough, Pecki. I can't stand any more of this."

I stamped out of the house, went to the movies by myself, and stayed there for three shows. Not really watching them but thinking instead. Thinking what I could do to turn my anger around. How to forgive myself and Paul. I remembered that Rusty had said that the energy for hatred and love were the same. When the movie house was closed, I came home and crept into bed beside Paul. In his sleep, he put his arm around me. The next morning I got up early to squeeze him fresh orange juice. I had been angry enough to think that I wanted to divorce him, yet there were homely things keeping us together: our bodies, our habits, our past and our animals.

Two days later, on August 27th, Tenzing died of a feline virus. He got sick on a Friday evening, our vet was away for the weekend, and, on Saturday, he didn't seem sick enough to go to a strange doctor; by early Monday morning, the conqueror of Everest was so weak that he couldn't jump onto the sofa. Even so, he asked to go outside. Several hours later, I found him half-way down the drive, lying on the grass, his gray-striped body already stiff. I took his lifeless bones, suddenly so light, into my arms and staggered up the drive under the weight of my tears. In his way, Tenzing had led us up the mountain. His love for both Josh and me had kept us together until we could begin to climb on our own.

Jonathan and I wrapped him in the afghan on Josh's bed

where he used to sleep, curled up into a soft furry ball, and buried him at the edge of the woods, piling enough rocks on his grave so that Sixer could not exhume him. We all grieved about him, but Paul and I could not stay home with our sorrow. Monday night was a regular meeting at the program. I debated about telling Josh that Tenzing was dead and decided to wait until he seemed emotionally stronger. He had quite enough to deal with now.

And Paul and I had our own problems. We were both exhausted and, in spite of my resolution, I was still angry. I tried to turn my emotional upheaval into more healthy channels, I went back to cultivating my friends. Often I would make arrangements to go somewhere with them, would be driving to wherever it was when I would find myself crying. The crying was cleansing and healing, and I accepted it as part of the release I needed. I knew I was crying from my soul.

I also made an appointment for an acupuncture tune up. This, I thought, would help me recover my balance and maintain my health.

"Your system has been ravaged," Dr. Rubin told me at the beginning of the treatment. "You are in such bad shape that we may have to go back to day-one and begin two treatments a week again."

"Whatever you say—I know I'm not in good emotional shape."

He listened to my pulses again and applied needles to the side of my face and neck. Then he turned off the light and left the room.

I was lying on the table thinking of nothing in particular when I suddenly saw black smoke pouring out of a window in the middle of my forehead. Billows of smoke were pouring out and rising up. I forced myself to picture a cloud whose puffy cheeks would blow away the smoke, but another picture came into my head. It was of the window of a row house in Philadelphia—a house like the one I lived in as a child—and from that window black smoke was pouring. The window became my third eye, and the smoke continued to billow. A thick growing black cloud settled above my head. I could not move it away. It grew larger and thicker and moved up and down with my breathing.

Suddenly, from my throat came an explosion, a mushroom cloud like the cloud of an atom bomb. The mushroom pushed through the dark cloud and began to break it up. From my heart, I saw flames shoot up and consume the dark mists above my head. Then everything disappeared and I ran my hands through my hair as if to shake out smoke.

When Dr. Rubin came into the room, I described what I had seen to him. He smiled, listened to my pulses, and said, "That's good. I'll see you in two weeks."

"So I'm better then? That blackness in me was released? It was a healing sent by God?"

"Through the meridian pathways," he said, smiling.

Later he told me that there is an acupuncture point called cloud gate in which he had placed a needle and that there are a series of points sometimes classified as windows in the sky. Someone who is closed in and cannot see the sun — like those in Plato's cave — can be helped to see it. Can be helped to look at the sky by needles in those points.

Chapter 18

Maple Tree

On our way to a weekly meeting at The Program one warm late September day in 1983, I was trying to read to Barbara an article on the use of cocaine amongst top traders on Wall Street from a *Wall Street Journal* that was flapping wildly and trying to fling itself through the open car window.

"They're doing a series," I said. "'High flyers,' they call them. 'Problem is rarely discussed, expert says, for fear of reaction by investors.'"

"*Newsweek* had a feature on drugs on the job," Barbara said. "The human and economic cost is enormous. Costs the economy billions of dollars, they said."

"That couldn't be the right figure, Barbara."

"It certainly is, Rich. I even remember the number 25.8 billion. They said drug use in the work place is as common as coffee breaks. Twenty-one guards at some nuclear facility were suspended for drug use, too."

"My God," said Paul. "We don't need to be blown up by the Russians."

"Every place I go now I hear or read about drugs. The secret epidemic isn't secret anymore."

Nobody disagreed, I guess, because we all sat in silence as the car sped down 95. I folded the newspaper, put it under my feet so that it wouldn't blow all over the car, and looked out at what I could see of the rich Maryland country-side along the highway. I thought of 95 as a double umbilical cord with me in the middle. At one end was Jonathan in school, at the other was Josh in the program. One kid at either end of a series of roadblocks and constructions which we and the Deavers negotiated weekly. Traveling the highway was time-consuming and exhausting but gave us plenty of opportunity to talk.

Mostly we talked about the program, its host parents, and how grateful we were to them for giving our kids a home. From the very first night, Josh and Andy had been taken by their assigned upper-phasers to stay with their families. "I really like them, Mom," Josh had told me last week. "They're nice to me."

"Please thank them for me. I know I'm not supposed to know who they are, but thank them for me anyway." I'll owe a debt to them, forever, I thought, aware that they had changed their lives to help their children and mine. They had accepted the responsibility for a locked house and an open heart. Children in the program were not institutionalized but lived in private homes where they were closely supervised by the upper-phaser who lived there too. Bedroom doors were locked every night to keep the newcomer from running away from the pain of breaking his druggy habits and learning to manage his mood swings in a normal manner.

"These stinking drives to Washington are nothing to what the host parents have to sacrifice in giving our kids a home," Rich said in one of our conversations.

"Some of the parents don't seem to think it's a sacrifice. At least, they say it's worthwhile because they see changes on a daily basis."

"Each child progresses differently, is different, in fact. The twelve steps allow for that."

"I've begun teaching ecology workshops to children for The Nature Center," I said. "Two days a week for the next few weeks, and you're right, they *are* all different. Some of the things they say you wouldn't believe."

That week I had taken a group of ten third graders to a

nearby park. We had sat on the ground under a large red maple, each child holding a maple leaf picked from the tree. I remembered the dialogue.

"Smell your leaf." I directed them. "Now put it in the palm of your hand. Look at it closely. Turn it over. Run your fingers along its veins. Measure its stem. Notice any special marks like spots or insect holes or tears."

"Mine has a bite in it," said one boy.

"Mine has a bug in a wooly blanket."

"Good. That will help you identify it. Now look at your leaf one more time, very carefully, and put it into this pile in the middle of our circle. That's right. Now that your leaf is in the pile, can you describe it?"

"Mine is big and green and has a torn edge."

"Mine had no stem."

"Mine had a long, long stem."

"Mine had a funny smell."

"Mine was just ordinary. I don't think I can find it again."

"Oh yes, you can. Everybody always finds the right leaf."

I stirred them with my hands and told the first child to pick out his leaf.

"This is mine. It has some red spots."

"So did mine. Maybe that's mine. Oh no, my leaf had more spots than that."

Each child in the circle was able to find his or her original leaf, even the little girl whose leaf was ordinary and looked like all the others.

"You see, each one of these leaves is different, but you can't tell that by looking up at the tree, can you?"

They all stared up into the green umbrella above them. "They look all alike," one boy said.

"But they're not. Isn't that right, Mrs. Sherman?"

"That's right. Each leaf is different—just like all of you. Together, you are all children, but each one of you is unique...Can anybody tell me what kind of tree this is?"

"It's a pine tree."

"No, silly. Pine trees are prickly. This tree has leaves. It's a oak."

"A oak, a oak!"

"No, guess again."

"I know, it's a swing tree. I mean, a maple tree like ours that's got a swing in it. My mom calls it the swing tree."

"You're right. It's a maple, and it will begin to turn a beautiful scarlet color in a few weeks."

"That was easy. I knew it was maple all along."

"Who can tell me what trees do for us?"

"They let us put swings on them."

"And they let birds sit on their branches."

"That's not helping people. Birds aren't people."

"But birds themselves help people. They eat insects. They plant seeds by dropping them. They..."

"They poop them too. My mommy told me so."

High up in the maple tree, a bird began a scrap of song, and a little boy cried out, "And they sing."

"What else do trees do for us?"

"They give us shade."

"And leaves to play in."

"And nuts."

"Some trees have pretty flowers."

"Some have berries 'n apples."

"Does a tree give us something that we use in our houses?"

"Wood. They give us wood."

"For furniture."

"And fires in our fireplace."

"Newspapers are made from wood too."

"What a smart group you are. Can you think of something else that a tree might do? It has to do with your nose."

"It makes stickers to put on your nose."

"Yes, and something else too. Everybody take a deep breath...Did that feel good?"

"Yes."

"The tree helps to purify the air that we breathe. It gives us oxygen and we give it carbon dioxide which helps its growth process. We and the trees work together to be healthy...Now who can tell me when a tree dies?"

"When somebody cuts it down."

"What happens to a tree when it's cut down?"

"It gets burned in the fire."

"It goes to a sawmill and is cut up."

"And then is it dead?"

"Yes, it's dead."

"No, it's not dead. It's a chair maybe."

"Well, when we burn it, it's dead."

"No, it's turned into energy when it's burned, and its smoke is carried on the wind. The energy is alive. It heats your house, and the ashes left from the fire can fertilize your garden."

"I know, a tree is dead if it's summer and it's got no leaves."

"But what if there are woodpeckers and squirrels and owls and insects living in that tree without leaves? Is the tree dead then?"

"If it falls down, it's dead."

"No, it's not. Things grow in it when it falls down, mushrooms 'n stuff.

"I'll tell you what I think. I think that a tree can go on living in a different form. There are violins made about three hundred years ago which are still playing beautiful music. They are still alive then, and they are made from the wood of trees which are alive in them, so that, although an individual tree may be cut down or may decay or may be burned, it's life — it's treeness, you might say — goes on in another form."

A little girl with brown pigtails, red leotards, and a freckled nose, jumped up, flung her arms around the maple as far as she could reach, and said, "I love you, tree."

"She's silly, isn't she, Mrs. Sherman?"

"No, she's not. An American Indian said that trees talk, they talk to each other, and they'll talk to you if you listen. Let's all go hug it and listen."

"I'm not gonna hug no tree."

But most of them did.

"You know," I told Barbara. "It's so nice. After one of my workshops, we walk back to the school waving good-bye to the trees, and one of the children always says to me. 'I'm so glad we didn't have school today, Mrs. Sherman.'

"That always tickles me, because actually they learned a lot. So did I. It's a matter of perspective, I guess."

"Yes. You showed the kids what they already knew about trees and the life force. Together, you opened windows, Pecki."

I thought of the window that had let out my black cloud and its accompanying burn-off of anger and fear, which was now beginning to seem more like a release of energy, the same kind of energy that the children understood as coming from the dead or dying tree and changing the pattern of its life force. In my case, the release of my anger in that black cloud allowed me to make a new pattern of thinking. It allowed me to admit my powerlessness over Josh.

Chapter 19

Coming Home

"The first thing to realize is that at a certain point when your child's drug habit is well established you have no power. No control over your child's drug problem." Barbara was speaking to a Parent-Teacher group at the local high school.

It was October, 1983. Nancy Reagan had begun her campaign to make the public aware of the seriousness of the drug problem, and Barbara and I were telling our stories to whatever group would listen. As the result of our public appearances, parents were coming to us with *their* stories, and, on our recommendation, many of them were either enrolling their children in The Program or joining self-help groups.

Our own children were still in the first phase of the program but were doing well. Josh was further along in the process of exposing his secrets, originally before the weekly meetings we all attended, and now to Paul and me and his peer group. Three quarters of his and any participant's time in The Program was spent in rap sessions which aimed at making the kids honest about their drug habits and behavior. Recently I had noticed a softening in his demeanor and a new clarity in his brown eyes. He stood straighter too, spoke more politely, and was taking on responsibility in the program, doing maintenance chores such as cleaning floors and washing windows. He had even been allowed to work near the doors — a sure sign that he was trusted not to run away.

On the third Friday in October, Paul and I arrived early enough at the meeting to get our favorite seats in the front row on the girls' side. I liked sitting there since I had gotten very interested in several of the children who sat across from me, and I could see them better from a front seat. That evening one of my favorite girls was sitting with her head sunk between shoulders rounder than ever, her fine red-gold hair falling over her face and shielding most of it from view. I could see, however, that she was chewing nervously on her lower lip. Every so often her seatmate would reach over and give her a quick little hug.

"That girl's had a set-back, I think," I said to Paul.

"Which girl?"

"The one in the third row—with the red-gold hair. See how flushed her face is."

"She doesn't look any too happy. Poor kid."

One of the staffers was on his feet. "We're beginning tonight's open meeting." The buzz in the room subsided, and the new children introduced themselves—as usual, making my heart ache. Then a boy and a girl, farther along in the program, spoke of their own progress, the result of both hard work and miracle, it seemed to me. Evidently Josh had benefited from neither, for when the leaders told all the boys to stand up who had earned the right to talk to their parents, he was not among them.

Now the microphone was circulating, coming first to us on the front row. I could think of nothing to say to Josh except that I was disappointed that he was not one of those who'd earned the right to talk to their parents.

"Josh, I'm so disappointed," I was beginning, when I heard his voice yell, "Coming home!" and his six-foot frame suddenly stood up in the middle of the group. As if he were carrying the ball to a touchdown, he ran across the space between the blocks of chairs, seized me, lifted me off my feet, hugged me, and in his excitement, did the same thing to Paul. Josh's face was radiant, cheeks pink, eyes flashing with pride and emotion. I, of course, cried, but, through my tears, was able to stumble out my thanks to the unknown parents who had been helping him all these months. Then I mumbled thanks to the staff and to Josh for all his hard work. Paul did the same.

That night we all three stayed in a room in a hotel—a little nervously, since good times together had not been a recent experience. I tossed and turned, and, in my tossing, heard Josh doing the same thing.

But in the morning, he was polite to the waiter, ate his breakfast with enjoyment, and had nice things to say— "The breakfast was good, the room was nice."—and, when we went out to get in the car, he stopped in his tracks to stare at a large Sweet Gum. "Gee, that's a beautiful tree. Yellow and scarlet stars. I don't remember seeing one like that before. But, then I didn't used to see things at all, did I? It's as if I've been—in the middle of a cloud, until now."

"You're coming out of it, Josh," I said, as we got in the car to make the nine-thirty deadline for being back in the building.

"I can tell you the name of my host family now, Mom. And I can talk to you on the telephone too. If you're here, we can even spend weekends together. Can you, Mom, Dad?"

"Yes, yes, yes," we said. This was the child who a few months previous would not have ridden in the same car with me. "We're so happy, Josh."

"When I make the next phase, I'll be able to start school."

"That's great, Josh. Do we need to sign you in? Will there be tuition?" Paul asked.

"I'll find out."

At the building, he said good-bye, got out of the car, and walked in by himself, turning at the door to smile and wave to us on the walk. Sunlight shone on his hair and shoulders like the crown and ermine he deserved, I thought, just before Paul and I both cried at his determination in going back into a situation so difficult and at ours in letting him do so. But, from other parents in the parking lot, we got nods and smiles of encouragement. They had been in our position too.

One good thing that had come out of the pain we'd been suffering was that Paul had learned to cry. Other men in the program had too. I noticed Army officers in their tunics and maple leaves crying in the parents' section, Navy officers in their stripes and gold braid crying too. But if the men were learning to be more vulnerable, the women seemed to be learning to be less so. At least, from the point of vulnerability to unhealthy emotional pressures. The women were learning not to be enablers, not to provide excuses for a non-functioning family.

In a few minutes we were back on the Beltway. The morning was typically October — clear, cool, sunny — and the traffic was gratifyingly sparse. We talked about meeting Josh's host parents, registering him in school, and where we would spend weekends with him near The Program. At least, he was back in the family again. "This time things will be different," Paul said. "Yes," I said. "I'm going to learn patience."

"Patience is a virtue, possess it if you can," I recited to myself, as at Havre de Grace we left 95 for Route 1, the scenic road by Star Roses, Longwood Gardens, Chadds Ford, and the Brandywine Museum. Just beyond Star Roses, I saw at an arm's reach in front of me, a large black heart. I felt it tugging at my chest, as if it was connected to me by a rubber band. I reached for it, took it in my hand, and felt it beating there, cradled between my two hands. There was a black shroud above it, and below it, there was black blood dripping.

"Paul, look." I pointed with one hand at the heart in my other, but he looked through the windshield at the road. "No, here. In the car. Do you see it? Do you see the black heart?"

"What black heart? Whose heart?"

"I think it's mine. Even though the heart in my chest is still there, it's connected to me. I can feel it tugging. It's black and it has a shroud and it's dripping black blood."

"Good God, Pecki. I hope you're imagining things."

"No, it's real. If I touch it, I can feel it beating."

"Well, it's some kind of vision then."

"Yes, I think it is. It is a vision. See if you can touch it too, Paul."

Paul waved his right hand around in front of me.

"Touch my hands. I'm cradling it." But even when he did, he felt nothing in them. "I don't feel anything there but your hands, Pecki."

"I'm holding it though. It's there, and I feel so sad. A kind of mourning—as if something is dead. Why do I feel that way? Why don't I feel happy instead? Here we are facing a new beginning with Josh, and I'm feeling as if it's an end."

"There's no way of getting back Josh's childhood again, Pecki. Perhaps that's what you're mourning. But it's gone. His childhood and adolescence are both gone."

"I know they are. I guess my heart is crying for them just the same. Black tears for the past, I suppose, but that's funny because there's not much of the last few years I'd want to save."

For about forty-five minutes, the heart continued to beat in my hands. I held it reverently and Paul continued to drive, neither of us talking. When it disappeared, I was left with a melancholy that lasted until the next morning, and then I found myself full of hope.

Chapter 20

Miracle Watching

So full of hope that it carried over into the talks Barbara and I were giving at schools and before women's and men's groups like the League of Women Voters, the Elks, and the Lions — and into a plan to give a dinner party. Emma Jean had been making me feel guilty about the 394.5 tomatoes still left to rot in my garden.

The next morning I picked enough tomatoes to make 5 quarts of green tomato soup and, on the spur of the moment, decided to invite some old friends to dinner that evening.

The dinner was delicious, if I do say so, the company should have been delightful, but, on the contrary, was depressing. Instead of fitting easily into my customary roundish niche in the familiar group, I found that I had become a square peg. I had new angles for which there was no place in that evening's conversation. It seemed as if the changes in Josh and in me, which I considered to be miracles, were only threats to them and their medical way of thinking about problems. Why didn't they want to hear about how acupuncture had helped me or how the crystal used by Mary Em had stopped my body's shuddering and released its terrible tension? Pecki, their resident health expert. Well, I was, whether they knew it or not. But after they laughed at me, I gave up trying to make them understand and sat at the table without talking, thinking of the night outside, of the trees and flowers and skies, which opened their arms to me, where I did fit in, square peg as I might be. The trees would applaud me and Paul and — particularly — Josh. They would applaud the hard work we all had done. I remembered from Isaiah: "The mountains and the hills shall break forth singing, and all the trees of the field shall clap their hands."

After they had all left and I was alone in the kitchen putting away the dishes, I thought over the conversation at the dinner table and realized that I would not be able to interest that particular kind of trained intelligence in holistic thinking. "Never mind, we love you anyway." Well, maybe. Listen to me was another thing.

Even for me, it had taken the psychic, Jean Hastings Quinn; Marianne Wolf and her dream workshop; Rusty Carnarius and her theories about body/mind energy; Rabbi Zalman and his confirmation of the Jewishness of the path I was following; Rosemont College and Therapeutic Touch; Sister Mary Em with her Soma and Visualization workshops; Peter Rubin and Acupuncture; and Josh's program of Straight to get me this far along the path I was following, I thought, as I threw the blue sponge with which I had been wiping counters into the sink. Of course, my dinner guests with their traditional medically-trained intelligence wouldn't be ready to reach my conclusions. Their paths weren't ready to go in my open windows.

For me, a new window had opened this week, and I was going through it. I was sitting in on an introductory workshop in Thymo-Kinesiology. Kinesiology, I was discovering, is a system of body-balancing through a series of muscle tests and corrections, the purpose of which is to eliminate stress — thus allowing restoration of energy flow — and to integrate body and mind, so that body/mind can communicate its needs.

"Here you are going off on another tangent," Paul had said when I told him about the new workshop.

"It's not another tangent, Paul. It's another application of the principles I've been following, the same principles used in Soma and Acupuncture."

"What principles are those, Pecki?"

"The principles of body/mind connection, of muscle/organ connection and response, the principle of a holistic approach to health and well-being. Body, mind, spirit, Paul. I'll explain more when you're ready to hear it, you jerk. Now I'm going to the workshop."

The leader of the workshop, Joan Hulse, had dark inquisitive eyes which she focussed on each of us in turn.

"Through my study of Applied Kinesiology and Holistic Health," she told us, "I've become fascinated with the ability of the body to communicate its needs. You will be too, I think."

"Now I'm going to show you how the body/mind reacts to language. May I have a volunteer?"

A strong-looking man in his thirties stepped up. Nautilus, I thought to myself.

"Stand relaxed, with your legs slightly apart," Joan directed. "Now raise your arm to the side on a level with your shoulder. Lock the joint. I will apply pressure above your wrist and push it down. Are you ready?"

The man flexed his muscle and said, "Yes."

"*Try* your best to resist me."

She laid her fingers above his wrist, pushed, and his arm went down. The young man looked mortified. In fact, he blushed.

"Now raise your arm again, lock your shoulder, and we'll do it once more."

Still looking embarrassed, he repositioned his arm.

"*Be* your best," Joan said, pushing at his arm exactly as she had done before.

This time the arm did not lower.

"What happened?" Joan asked.

"I don't know. I didn't try any harder."

"It's the word 'try.' 'Try' has a negative effect. It introduces stress into a situation and actually saps a person's strength. When the verb 'be' is used, the body/mind is integrated and strengthened."

"That's hard to believe," said Nautilus. "Let's do it again." He held up his arm, looking more determined than ever.

"Try your best," said Joan.

Again his arm collapsed at her pressure, and again he blushed.

"Raise your arm again, lock your shoulder. Now *be* your best." This time his arm held steady. There was a surprised murmur in the room.

"Choose a partner and see for yourselves," Joan directed.

I found that her claims about the body's reaction to the two verbs were quite correct. When I was told to *try*, I couldn't, and when I was told to *be*, my arm remained upright and steady.

"When you hear the verbs 'try' and 'be', it's your body/mind that's listening. I wanted you to experience this for yourselves before we went on with the demonstration."

I thought of what Allen Maller had said in his book on the Kabbalah that YHVH, the word for God, is based on the Hebrew for "to be." He said that the tense of YHVH is causative. "God is he who causes to be. God is the potentiality of the future." So when someone says "be" to somebody else, that someone is touching the God-sense, and the body/mind recognizes the rightness of that.

"The Army must have caught on too," I told the class. "Their slogan is, 'Be all that you can be.'" We all laughed.

"We have a friend here today, somebody as new to me as she is to you," Joan now said, "who is going to allow us to illustrate what happens when there is a break in body/mind integration. Betsy, will you tell us a little bit about the last few years of your life?"

"Nine years ago," said Betsy, "while I was in college, I was giving a golf lesson. I told my pupil never to swing his club unless he was sure there was no one close by. However, he forgot, raised his nine iron and hit me on the side of the head. A witness told me later that the impact threw me across the green. I was unconscious and in a coma for many months. In the hospital, I had to be taught to walk, talk, eat, and read all over again. I am now married and back in school, but it's tough."

"Will you walk for us, Betsy?"

Betsy walked stiffly across the room, looking to me as if she'd been programmed. Her facial muscles were tense, her jaw seemed to be clenched, and I noticed that she did not swing alternate arms as her legs moved, but only slightly moved the arm on the same side as the leg with which she was taking a step.

Joan then asked her to follow a pencil with her eyes while it was moved in front of her face. She had to turn her whole head in order to do so.

"Now get on the table, Betsy."

"All right, but I don't know what to expect."

"I'm going to do some muscle testing and strengthening exercises. When I start to lift your left leg, resist me." Joan seemed to lift the leg easily, however, and moved around the table to lift the right one. "Oppose me, Betsy. That's fine. Through these tests, your body is telling us (and you) its needs and is signaling to your brain." She pumped Betsy's leg up and down. "What corrections we are doing work on both sides of the body and in the brain. Moshe Feldenkrais, a physicist and engineer and a Master in Judo, became interested in body/mind mechanics. He said, 'So smart is the brain when we permit it that even after doing something wrong a million times, doing it right once feels so good that the brain/body recognizes it immediately.'

"That's what we're doing with Betsy—some things that are right, which her body/mind will recognize and accept," Joan told the class.

"That leg feels stronger against your pushing," Betsy said.

Joan moved from Betsy's legs to her arms, following the same procedures of lifting and pumping, sometimes vertically and sometimes to the side, which reminded me of Touch for Health. She worked slowly and methodically moving from right to left, from top to bottom of Betsy's body. After about a half-hour, Joan walked slowly around the end of the table and placed her fingers on Betsy's forehead. Suddenly Betsy's body whipped towards the left side of the table and she gave a terrible moan. The friend who had brought Betsy to the workshop caught hold of her feet so that she wouldn't fall. She continued moaning and sobbing in a way that brought tears to the eyes of everyone in the room, while Joan kept her hands lightly on Betsy's forehead.

Someone in the room began to chant, "ohm." Everyone joined in, and the sound vibrated from all corners of the room, through all our bodies, subsiding at last, but not dying. The vibrations of that ohm were retained in our body/mind, I was sure of that.

Betsy was now lying in a relaxed manner on the table, her eyes open and her ears wet with tears.

"Do you feel like sitting up, Betsy?" Joan asked.

She sat up slowly, her shoulders hunched, her legs dangling over the edge of the table, and tears still streaming from her eyes. Suddenly, she started rolling her hands around on her wrists, and then her feet on her ankles. A broad grin filled her face. Her jaw was relaxed, I noticed. She opened and closed her mouth and swiveled her jaw from side to side. All of us had begun clapping for her, and Betsy's eyes which had been bright with tears were even brighter with delight.

"What happened, Betsy?" Joan asked.

"I relived the accident. I experienced the pain I hadn't felt before."

"That must have been horrible," I said.

"It was—but it was wonderful too. Look at me, I can roll my hands and feet. I haven't been able to do that for nine years."

"Can you walk across the room now, Betsy?"

Betsy jumped from the table and stepped out, swinging

her arms with the alternate legs, walking like the graceful athlete she was, not like the programmed robot she had been half an hour ago. We clapped again.

Joan then held the pencil in front of Betsy's eyes, moved it from side to side, and Betsy's eyes—not her head—followed it.

"That's wonderful. A miracle." Even Nautilus said so.

"Before you leave, Betsy, I'll give you some exercises you must do to continue the corrections you've begun," Joan said. "Now we're going to do an exercise that we can all share. It's called emotional stress release. May I have a volunteer?"

I raised my hand.

"Pecki," she said, reading my name tag, "sit in front of me. I'm going to place my hands on your forehead while you think of a stressful situation you've been involved in."

I sat down in the chair, she moved behind me, touched my temples gently with her fingers, and asked me to concentrate on a bad situation and run the scene of it through my head. I decided to think of the time Josh almost pulled a knife on me. I watched him walk in the front door, with his chains and knife and dirty bandanna. I saw his teeth clench and hate flash in his eyes. I watched the afternoon light glint on the chain around his leg and the studs in his jeans. I saw my own back as I turned it to walk into the kitchen. I saw him following me. I saw all six feet of him, the great muscles in his arms, and my nose level with his chest. Then I saw Sara walk into the room and ask for a cup of tea.

"Stop the picture, Pecki. Now rewind it."

That was very hard to do. I moved back from Sara, through the afternoon sunlight, to Josh in his chains at the front door.

"Now picture a happy scene with the same person, if you can. If you can't, any happy scene will do."

Josh was a toddler. It was fall and he and I were planting bulbs where they could be easily seen from the kitchen window...And then I reprogrammed the scene. Certainly there had been more recent happy times with him than that. I thought of the time we had gone for ice cream to celebrate his home run that had won the Little League game for his team. Then I thought of even a better time, the time I went to his school to take him out for lunch — just because I loved him and wanted to give him a special treat. We went to the Rusty Scupper, and he ordered spareribs, spreading grease all over his broad smile. We said hello to those businessmen lunching around us who happened to be Paul's friends and talked and laughed. I was proud of Josh's healthy, handsome, friendly face, his clear eyes, and the loving way he was looking at me. We enjoyed each other then.

"Now replay your first scene, Pecki."

I did. The anger and fear were gone.

It was a miracle that I could achieve for myself. With hard work, of course. But then didn't most miracles take hard work? Certainly Betsy's had. Hard work and readiness to accept it. I'd been ready, ready to give up my terror and hatred of Josh. It was a miracle I'd been ready for.

Rusty had said that good and evil use the same energy. It's a matter of how it's used, not a matter of a different supply. Just as the poppy can be used for good and evil: for drug addiction and for alleviating suffering. In medicine, opium is the most effective pain reliever known, but, improperly used, it is both physically and psychologically addictive.

My energy also had its good and bad sides. I had been using it to hate Josh, to wish for his death and mine, even to plot his murder. Now I was beginning to feel the shift, beginning to use that same energy to heal him and myself. To lead us both to life, not death. The black heart was gone and in its place was a healthy heart made whole, I thought, partly by the months of repetition of that "Love ya" refrain in the program, which somehow succeeded in opening me to the real thing. All the time the love had been there like the spot in the Yin-Yang symbol, the seed of white in the black half. But, of course, that's not the whole of it. There's a seed of black in the white half too. Each half has a seed of the other, and both halves are needed to make the whole.

I wondered if I could tell Josh or Jonathan about what I was learning, whether they would listen, and was afraid that the answer was, fat chance. Even so, I'd found my own miracle and went home that evening full of enthusiasm. I told Paul about Betsy and was pleased with his astonished face.

That night I dreamt that *my house, a small house, in a small town, was for sale. I was showing it to a family interested in buying it. I took them through the rooms, sometimes opening closet doors and finding behind them apartments I'd forgotten were there. Then I took them out to the screen porch to show them the small green lawn. A gray spot appeared in the grass. As we watched it, it turned into an elephant. Soon there were many elephants, and the grass had turned to mud. We went back into the house, I thinking that I'd better get one of the dogs to control the elephants. Through a side window, I saw a part-hippo part-elephant emerging from the mud. It had a stubby elephant's trunk. The lawn began to undulate in waves, and the child of the family became frightened.*

I woke up, wrote down my dream and analyzed it. The house, of course, was me, the forgotten rooms were unknown resources. Although I'd dreamed of an elephant before — its first appearance had been as an elephant's trunk — its meaning as a symbol was not clear to me. The mud seemed to mean that there were still things to be cleaned away. Perhaps the elephants coming up through it meant that there was something strong and powerful underneath that had to be dealt with. The child in me was frightened, and it was clear that the house in its present condition could not be sold. I was not ready to leave it behind.

Chapter 21

No Short Cut

Nor was Josh ready to leave his host family, even though his host brother, David, had now graduated from the program. David's family wanted Josh to stay on, in spite of the restrictions and requirements which would be placed upon their household because of the new children in The Program who would be brought there to live with Josh as an upper-phaser: restrictions such as locked doors and requirements such as time spent driving back and forth to the program and to Josh's school in another area, waiting around sometimes as long as an hour while Josh fulfilled certain duties within the building — organizing meetings, attending rap sessions, etc. — and twice-a-week evening meetings which they had to attend because of his presence in their house and/or Josh had to be driven to. With all those extra problems they still wanted him to stay, but, shortly after the New Year in 1984, the Senior Staff told Josh that he would have to find a new place to live.

"It's not fair to David and his family to be so restricted now that David's graduated, Josh."

"Yeah, you're right. But where can I go?"

"There are other families with upper-phasers who will be glad to have you."

"Okay."

"You must be ready to move in two weeks."

"Okay."

But Josh didn't want to ask another family to take him. Instead, he asked me to move down. "We can live together, Mom."

I was flattered that he wanted to live with me, but annoyed that he would not consider the inconvenience he would be causing the rest of us. I would be leaving my home and husband, Paul would be losing his wife, and Jonathan would be missing a mother when he came home on weekends. Paul, of course, was opposed to the plan, the staff thought it was unnecessary, but Josh's host mom said, "It's a good chance to mend fences, Pecki."

That and a dream made up my mind for me.

I dreamt that *Paul and I were going to the program to pick up Josh. Paul, who was driving my car, took a short cut around the back of the gas station near the building. I realized that this was not possible, but as we rounded a dumpster, a sturdy man with no legs, seated on a small dolly, called to us. Paul did not stop. The man grabbed the handle on my side of the car, pulled open the door, and seized my ankle. He was strong enough to prevent the car from moving forward.*

I woke up, wrote down the dream, and worked on it till dawn. It seemed obvious that the dream was telling me that I had turned over my power of decision to Paul (he was driving my car), that there was really no short cut to where I wanted to go to, and that someone who was crippled was asking for my help. Ah-ha. I decided to go.

In the morning, I told Paul.

"There's no sense arguing with your dream, Pecki," he said, "but you won't find any place to live anyway, so I'm not worrying."

He was wrong. I found a two-bedroom apartment in the Alexandria area, on a three-month sublet. By February 1st, 1984, Josh and I had moved in.

During the three month period that we were living there, besides the two of us, there were occasionally as many as six others. Most of the time, whoever was there was involved with The Program and school, but occasionally we could work in some fun time. The problem was what kind of fun. We would have liked to have gone to the movies more often, but there were few suitable films for Josh and the others to see. Two hits were *Risky Business* and *The Big Chill*. In *Risky Business*, the protagonist gets involved with drugs, a prostitute, and the bribery of a University alumnus whose job is to recommend candidates for admission. In the film, every shoddy thing that the student does works out well for him. His use of marijuana gets him in no trouble, his sex acts contract no diseases, he is never exposed to his parents, and is accepted in the college of his choice, Princeton. It was hardly the kind of success story that I wanted Josh to see.

In *The Big Chill*, a group of 60's graduates come together for the funeral of one of their classmates and share drugs, alcohol, and bed-hopping. The movie is a well-acted presentation of life in the 80's, perhaps, but again, it was not one that I thought Josh was ready to see, since it portrays its various addictions as normal — even acceptable — behavior. (We could enjoy *Splash*, however, another hit about a mermaid who, for a short time, turns into a woman. True love, a happy ending, lots of sex, but no addictions.)

Television presented the same problem: How to find programs that didn't present drinking or pill-popping as a way to achieve well-being. In the case of beer commercials, the observer is led to understand that a brew is the best way to have fun, share camaraderie, gain success — both social and sexual — and become macho. No wonder so many of the young become drinkers. And the pill-popping ads, advocating a cute little pill for your constipation, headache, acid indigestion, arthritis, insomnia, and drowsiness encourage an acceptance and quite unnecessary reliance upon over-the-counter drugs.

The advertising industry message is telling the public to rely on panaceas for any problem from bad breath to hemorrhoids.

Our difficulties with the entertainment media led us to

spend considerable time in the Smithsonian, particularly in the Air and Space Museum, and, weather permitting, in walking around the city often between the Washington Monument and the Lincoln Memorial. We also spent time standing at the Vietnam Wall, touching the names with our fingers and being touched by them in return.

On the weekend of the sixth of March, Josh and I went home for Sixer's birthday and for an acupuncture treatment for me. Spring had come to Washington, and I needed reinforcement against its pollen and fragrances. It was our first trip home, Jonathan came home too, and we celebrated Sixer's birthday with ice cream and cake which he ate out of a bowl on the floor. We spent most of the time in the kitchen, around an enormous pot of vegetable soup and a continuous blaze in the wood-burning stove. I was very happy to be home and to have my bed, pillow, and partner back again.

On Sunday night, Josh and I drove back to Virginia. We got caught in another traffic jam. I clenched the steering wheel, gritted my teeth, and recited the serenity prayer:

God grant me the serenity

To accept the things I cannot change,

The courage to change the things I can,

And the wisdom to know the difference.

"Oh, Mom," Josh said, and sighed.

"If I can apply that to this situation, I can apply it anywhere . . . even to the fights we have sometimes, Josh."

"They've been good fights, Mom. At least, the recent ones."

"Yes, I've been learning to let go, haven't I? And learning to listen too. Am I listening enough now?"

"No, but you're getting there."

A few days after we were back in Alexandria, we were invited to become speakers for The Program. Speaking was nothing new to me, since Barbara and I had been doing a lot of it before community groups, but Josh and the others were nervous. Nevertheless, they did very well. They were honest and candid in answering questions from the audience, who seemed to have a little trouble jibing their healthy young American appearance with their drug history. "I can't believe you were really on all those drugs," was a comment we heard frequently. "But I was — and I used drugs in school too." "Did your teacher know it?" "Yes, I did drugs with the teacher. Even my psychiatrist offered to." There was a gasp of horror from the audience, some of whom were occasionally a little tipsy at the dinner meetings. This was a matter of amusement to our group who felt it odd that parents who were looking for information on their children's drug use would be using one themselves. Alcohol is a drug, of course, and can lead to addiction.

On the way to one of our presentations, Susan, who was just about to graduate from the program, told me about a recent dream. She was running from her old druggy friends when she came to a river spanned by an old railroad trestle. She started across it but came to a section where there were no ties under the rails but only the water rushing along below. She was determined to cross anyway, determined to get away from her druggy friends who were trying to draw her back into their addiction, but it was a big gap, and the rails looked too narrow and slippery to walk. She got ready to jump, not at all sure that she could reach the ties on the other side. Just then, up from the water came a friend from The Program. He placed his shoulder in a convenient spot for her foot, and, with that help, she was able to leap across. When she turned around to thank him, he had disappeared.

"Wasn't that a funny dream, Mrs. Sherman?"

"A wonderful dream. It shows that the people of The Program are there to help you when they're needed."

In that dream, she had passed another test, evidently. I realized that these kids were being tested everywhere: at home, in school, and even in their dream lives. They needed to learn and practice the skills for living which they had missed learning earlier. Because they had taught themselves to alter their moods through drugs, they had missed most of the lessons usually learned during adolescence, how to study, how to accept disappointment, how to treat friends, how to love and be loved. They didn't know how to adjust to hormonal swings, therefore, they didn't know how to handle their moods in normal situations. They had to learn that they were worthwhile people whose negative energy could be switched to positive forms.

Spring was really in Washington now. The Tidal Basin drifted in cherry blossoms. It was very beautiful, but I was anxious to get home. I missed Paul. Often we called each other three or four times during the day. Our dialogue had distinct overtones of puppy love, perhaps, but the real love was underneath, and I wanted to be with him. Since Josh had found a new host family, who felt that he would be a good example to their son and were anxious for him to move in, on April 28th, I packed my things, closed the apartment, and set off for home.

On the way, I thought of my Jackson Pollock puzzle and that most of its pieces had now fallen into place. Not completely, of course. There were missing pieces here and there, holes that represented lots of struggle still ahead, but struggle that my good electricity was going to help, struggle that I could win by not *trying* but by *being*. By practicing *being* with all that I'd learned about body/mind.

Lavender lilacs greeted me as I drove in the driveway. And pink dogwoods and white and pink flowering apple and peach trees. I parked the car, and was welcomed hysterically by Sixer, Dubie, and Feather and Scratchie, the cats.

Before going into the house, I, of course, visited the gardens, the blue flowers of the Jacob's Ladder, the coral bells, and the white violets in the lawn. I smelled the gingery fragrance of the white viburnum by the stone wall. I said hello to everything, stooping down to pat here and there a particularly appealing bloom, looking up to admire the new emerald leaves on the trees.

"If I keep a green bough in my heart, the singing bird will come," I recited to myself.

Paul arrived with a large bag of Chinese food. We ate out

of the boxes in the kitchen and grinned at each other.

That night I dreamt *that I was in a strange underground cavern (not dark), the walls of which glowed pink. In the cavern, there was a beach of pink sand and a clear pool of water. My legs were in the water up to the calf, but I had a feeling that even though I was standing on the bottom, the water was deeper than that. Around my legs swam brilliant tropical fish. A fish net appeared in my hand. I put it into the water and caught a perfectly-formed small elephant. "An elephant isn't a fish," I said in my dream. I took it out of the net and cuddled it in my hand. Then I noticed other miniature elephants swimming around my legs.*

Chapter 22

A Clear Path

Whether or not I knew what the elephant meant to me as a dream symbol, it was now whole and small enough for me to handle. Like our family situation, I wondered — manageable, no longer in parts or muddied? The water in the dream was deeper than I thought it was, but I felt quite comfortable standing in it, even though conscious of unseen depths.

In my waking life, the water was deeper than I thought it was too. I found that out in a disturbing conversation with Josh, which I decided to report to the staff in a call to the program.

"When I asked Josh on the phone yesterday about school, he said, 'What do you care?' Something's wrong, I think. I don't know what it is, but something's wrong with Josh," I told the staffer.

"Thank you, Mrs. Sherman. We'll look into it and call you tomorrow."

Tomorrow wasn't soon enough to resolve my anxiety. I called Josh's host mom and talked for two hours — good soul that she was to listen to me.

She agreed that something was wrong. "There's nothing I can put my finger on, Pecki, but Josh is withdrawing. It's his attitude. It's not that he isn't helpful as always, but he's less cheerful, evasive even somehow. When we talk to him now, he looks away. I'm glad you reported it."

I hung up the phone, more disturbed than ever, and

went out to the garden to pull up the masses of jewel weed growing behind the bird feeder. "Oh, God," I said, pulling out a handful. "Something's wrong. Is he taking drugs again?" I seized a few more weeds, and then apologized to them for cutting short their lives. They were so green and healthy and full of juice and full of the promise of their yellow and orange flowers. As I was full of promise before Josh had called. Now, like the jewel weed, I'd been dragged up by my roots. "Forgive me," I said to the flowers as I reached for some more to pull. Six inches from my hand was a poison ivy vine. I am highly allergic to it, but jewel weed is its antidote, and my hands were covered with their juice. Another case of Yin-Yang, I thought to myself, of the positive and negative making the whole if you know where to look for it. The analogy should have been healing, but I was not healed by it. I had allowed myself to slip back into a crisis mentality, had forgotten my new-found wholeness, my ability to keep the elephants of my life in balance. I was back in my old pattern of destructive emotion, and Josh was back in his, as staff told me when they called.

"You were right to trust your gut feelings, Mrs. Sherman. We confronted Josh and found out that he's been cutting classes. Some of the kids had been making fun of him for being in the program. But instead of talking about the problem with one of us, he kept it a secret, cut class, and is now feeling guilty. That is what caused his evasive and rude behavior to you and his host mom."

"What'll happen to him now?"

"We'll pull him into the full rap sessions."

"What does that mean?"

"We'll keep him out of school for a few days, put him in group, let him talk it out, and get back on the track. He won't be staying with his host family until he's being honest again."

I had twisted the telephone cord into so many knots that I had to bend over to talk in it. "I'm glad you caught it. Let me know how he progresses," I said and started to hang up when I heard the staff member say, "Don't worry. I had four setbacks in my program. What we say around here is that from regression comes growth."

However, that was not Josh's only regression. A few months later, when he was much farther along in The Program, there was a far worse one.

He had completed staff training, was nearing graduation, and had gone with us to Bermuda for the week's family vacation that The Program recommended as a prerequisite to graduation. It was August, and we snorkeled, rode motor bikes — somehow being able to stay on the left side of the road — played golf and tennis, and basked on the beach. The water was turquoise and aquamarine. Tropical fish (though no elephants) swam around our legs. There was always a breeze blowing pungent tropical scents, and there was always a meal being served. When we got home, Josh was to drive himself back to The Program and his host family, but he told us that he didn't want to go.

"I know how to stay drug-free now, Mom. I'll stay here and go to a self-help program. I don't need Straight anymore."

"Oh, no, Josh," said Paul. "It's time you finished something that you've begun. You haven't done that for a long while and you're going to finish The Program."

"But..."

"There's no buts about it."

"I'm not going back, Dad. That's all." I saw that he was crying.

"If you don't go, Josh, don't think you're going to live with us. We won't have you here until you graduate. You probably only have a few weeks more. Go back, Josh. Complete the program and you have a family. Don't, and you don't. We love you more than ever, but we're not letting you — or ourselves — slip up now."

Paul was now crying too, and so was I. We were all crying, but in spite of our anguish, the conversation was calm and loving and quite different from those held earlier, in that we all, Josh, Paul, and I, were taking responsibility for our actions and would suffer our own consequences.

Josh turned on his heels and walked down the driveway, leaving us crying but determined not to back down. Wherever he went, he did not come home that night. Even though Paul and I were aware that we might never see Josh again, we spent the evening, still calm and determined, and more than ever loving. I kept repeating for both our benefits, "Remember, we have control only over ourselves and our own actions, not over Josh and his."

That night I had a dream.

In my dream, *it was morning and I woke up early to let out the dogs. When I opened the door, I saw snow and ice. The driveway, however, was clear. I asked myself why the dogs hadn't barked at the noise of the snowplow, and why it hadn't awakened me. Then I saw three women walking up the drive towards me. I recognized the middle woman as a friend. She was the mother of two children and a marathon runner, red-headed, smiling, humorous, and healthy. I saw that the three women were walking easily up the cleared drive.*

When I woke up, I thought about the dream and realized that my friend represented health and well-being. I realized too, that those three women represented the three parts of me: body, mind, spirit — all in good health and walking easily along the path, now cleared by the work I had done.

Twenty-four hours later, Josh walked up the driveway and knocked on the front door. Paul and I both stepped out on the terrace.

"Where did you spend the last two nights, Josh?"

"In the woods."

"Are you hungry?" I asked.

He nodded his head, so I brought out a tray with granola, milk, fresh-squeezed orange juice, blackberries from the edge of the woods and peaches from our trees. I set it down on an iron table. While he was eating, I told him my dream. He seemed to understand what it said to me: that I was healthy, that my path was clear.

"Have you used drugs since you left here?" Paul asked him.

"No, not even a cigarette."

"I love you, Josh, but unless you complete the program, I won't have anything further to do with you," I said, turning and going into the house.

Two hours later, Paul called me to come from where I'd been hovering in the kitchen. The two men were sitting on black iron chairs on the terrace. Josh's face was flushed, but the look that he gave me out of his brown eyes was clear and controlled. "I'm ready to go, Mom. Will you and Dad please come with me?"

We did.

When we went through the Baltimore tunnel and were close to Washington, the three of us found ourselves crying again. It had been a painful decision for Josh to make. He would probably have to go back to day-one in the program, have to repeat all the steps he had already taken, be held by the belt loop again wherever he went.

"It was a tough decision, wasn't it, Josh? Going back, taking on The Program again?"

"Yes, I sure don't want to. But I knew I had to make a choice between you and Dad or having no family at all if I quit."

"But why on earth did you decide not to go back?"

"I didn't exactly mean to. I just wanted to stay home, go to school, and be normal for a change."

"Normal can be finishing things — and you're not. Not finishing things was your pattern, Josh," said Paul.

"I guess I want to do things my way, Dad. That's always been my trouble, hasn't it?"

"You test the system, and that's not always good. Sometimes your tests go too far and sometimes you test where even one experiment brings disaster," I said.

"It's not just systems you're testing, Josh. Not just systems that you want to expose as unreasonable and unjust and inapplicable to you. Not systems that you don't trust. It's yourself too. You have to learn to recognize that."

We said good-bye in the office, hugging and kissing and crying some more. Even so, there was a calmness prevailing over the scene, a calmness in us.

As for me, my paths were integrating. I was no longer being pulled along one that was dark and desperate and forever dropping. That path had rejoined the other, the one of my alternate methods of health, and the two paths together continued to move upward, brighter, more hopeful, full of messages of joy and strength. Where did those messages come from? They came from me. (Doesn't the Koran say that the Universe is as close as the veins in your neck?) From my good electricity, from nature, from God. I bend my knee in gratitude and love.

> To bow and bend we will not be ashamed
> To turn to turn
> T'will be our delight
> Till by turning, turning we come round right.

Postscript

"There's Nothing as Whole as a Broken Heart"

It took us the next seven months to begin to "come round right." During that time, I continued acupuncture and was active in Al-Anon, and for the first time in five years, spent a serene and healthy winter at Sporting Hill Farm. In that same amount of time, Josh completed the Program — a record — and began to work as a Junior Staffer (a paid position at Straight) while finishing high school. Before those seven months were over, he called us to say that he had been invited by the attorney for the Presidential Commission on Organized Crime to testify in their investigation of cocaine use. His name had been suggested by the Program. He would be on television broadcasting his story nationwide, and that was more public than he was ready to be. Still he wanted to do what he could to raise citizen awareness of the drug problem. It was a hard decision for him, but he decided to say yes. So, when the attorney for the Commission called to ask Paul's and my permission, we gave it immediately.

The morning of his testimony, Josh, his host family, and I arrived at a large gray building in Washington, were searched, tagged, and escorted to a room where we were told to await the Counsel for the Commission.

He walked in with two FBI agents, who were there to reassure us that we were quite safe. (How's that for making you nervous?) "We'd better leave while the going's good," Stan, Josh's host brother, whispered to me. I could see that

Josh was ready to walk out. He was tapping the wooden arm of his chair, pounding the floor with one foot, and pulling at his collar. In spite of his nervousness, he looked very handsome in a soft blue tweed jacket, navy slacks, and his dad's red paisley tie. I thought that he looked older than his not quite eighteen years.

When we were taken into the large hearing room, we were dismayed to see what felt like a large crowd: twelve committee members, Senator Strom Thurmond and Judge Irving Kaufman as co-chairmen, sitting behind a long curved table, two attorneys sitting in front of them, a small audience, and banks and banks of television cameras. Josh's host family and I were seated behind the table where Josh sat with the other witnesses.

After introducing him to the Commissioners, the attorney asked Josh to tell them what drugs he had been using. He went over the old list. "Cocaine, pot, alcohol, hash, hash oil, LSD, mushrooms, ludes, nitrous oxide, rush, and Thai sticks. I think that's all." There was a gasp in the hearing room.

"Did you ever steal from your family, Josh?" the attorney asked.

"Yes, I stole my mother's silver. I stole money from her pocketbook, and I stole stuff from my friends' families."

"Did you ever attack your mother, Josh?"

"No, but I almost did. I threatened her with a knife."

Josh's voice was tight and controlled. I could see him struggling for honesty.

"Sometimes, I wanted to see her dead. No, not me really, the drugs wanted to see her dead." His voice was shaking, and I found myself crying again that this fine-looking child of mine had suffered such degradation and pain. Crying not only for him, but for myself too. The degradation and pain hadn't been his alone.

"How did you get to the Program, Josh?" Counsel was asking.

"My parents tricked me. Else I wouldn't have gone."

"When you were taking all those drugs, would you have overdosed, would you have taken an unlimited amount of cocaine if it had been available to you?"

"Yes. Yes, I would've."

"Even if it killed you?"

"Yes."

"Would you now?"

"No." Josh's jaw was thrust out and the "no" came out strong and loud. Beside me, the host mother was now crying, and my teeth had started to chatter. In the background the cameras were whirring, focusing sometimes on Josh, sometimes on me, sometimes on Strom Thurmond, and sometimes on the Commissioners.

For forty-eight hours afterwards that scene ran on CNN television and was picked up by the major networks as well.

As soon as I got home from Washington, the phone began to ring. Calls from all over the country came in, both to give us support and to tell us their stories. Here was a chance for us, in our turn, to try to help others, to try to repay those parents who had taken Josh and Paul and Jonathan and me into their homes and hearts. We could not repay them directly but we could give the same gifts to others who needed them.

I was particularly interested in the mothers; most of them needed to be told they were not going crazy and that their feelings and fears were actually there.

"You're not imagining it," I would say, "you're not going crazy but there may not be much you can do for your child right now. Why not concentrate your energies on yourself? What do you need? What would make you feel better?" Very few of them could answer that, so I would suggest Tough-Love and Al-Anon. "That's where you'll get the support you need," I told them, finding my own burden lightened with every bit of help I was able to give these others. Often, when I was on the telephone, I felt a spurt of my good electricity and knew that some kind of a connection had been made. I had helped the person I was talking to. That person was trusting me. There was a give-and-take in the process: my good electricity spurted, my dream life became active, and that was helping me process my past. One of the dreams that seemed particularly significant took place on a February night in 1985.

I dreamt that *Paul, Jonathan, and I were vacationing in a condo at the seashore. I was alone in our 10th floor apartment when I felt that I needed some fresh air and exercise. Without thinking twice about it, I opened the window and stepped out on a ledge running around the building. Somehow the height didn't bother me, but, in trying to maneuver around a protruding girder, I pulled the marble window sill I was clinging to loose. Together we plummeted backwards towards the ground. I was terrified. I told myself to relax and to breathe deeply in order to minimize injury. As we fell, the marble window sill lying across my chest turned into a foam rubber bolster, and I landed on the sand with it lying lightly upon me. Nevertheless, I felt that my back was broken. I saw Paul and Jonathan walking along the beach, chatting together, their arms joined, but their backs towards me, and quite oblivious to my cries for help.*

A lady and a cat approached. We talked about the cat as it nuzzled me, and I suggested that she go for help. When she didn't return, I dragged myself to a beach house — white walls, sun, and a phone on the floor, but I could get no answer on it to any of my calls. I then remembered the goldfinch I had seen at the birdfeeder that morning and that, at first, I had thought I would like to have a yellow bird in a cage and, later, that I didn't want anything at all caged. "No cages." As I said that in my dream, I felt a small bird in my hand, its heart beating fast against my palm. "If I keep a green bough in my heart, the singing bird will come." When I pulled myself into another room of my dream beach house, Paul was there.

"Paul, my back hurts, lie on my back," I said, as I woke up aching.

"Later, Pecki," he said, turning over.

That week, I told my dream to Marianne's dream group.

"Stepping out a tenth floor window? You certainly believe in taking risks, Pecki."

"The marble window sill turned into a foam bolster. You were bolstered," somebody pointed out.

"Could your broken back be a break from the past — past/back, a play on words perhaps?" Marianne asked me.

"Yes, oh yes," I said. "And the singing bird was a gift, wasn't it? A gift that I can give to others."

A few days later, there was a phone call from Hollywood asking for a kind of a gift. A producer wanted to film our story. We talked it over. I said, yes, it would help others, but Josh, Jonathan, and Paul said, no. So that was the official answer. Nevertheless, the idea of telling the story stuck in my head. I had kept journals, so why not do a book? There was plenty of drama, yes, and growth too. My elephant dreams were clear evidence of that. They'd been progressing from a piece of an elephant (the trunk) to imperfect, unwelcome ones (elephants which erupted on my lawn and prevented me from selling my house — or me) to a perfect though miniature elephant I could hold in my hand almost like the singing bird. Perhaps there were more elephants still to come and further answers to my problems.

I kept turning over in my head the problem of the book. I wasn't a writer. I would need somebody to help me and it would have to be two stories: the story of Josh's addiction and what happened to all of us because of that, and the story of my growth in awareness and health, the miracle of understanding that my awkward, skeptical feet were stumbling upon. A miracle that was not yet complete. There was further work to be done — I knew that — and a phone call from Phyllis Popkin presented the next step in my education.

"Pecki, I'm so proud of you, darling. I saw you on CBS last week. You were wonderful, and there's something I want you to do with me. Come to the Gateway Program at the Monroe Institute.

"But what is it, Phyllis?"

"It's a workshop on integration of the right and left hemispheres of the brain through sound waves."

"Well . . . what does that do?"

"Makes your brain stop arguing with itself and start working as a whole. That gives you a much deeper sense of awareness. You find out what's right for you, and your life gets happier. It's worked for us. Arnie's practice is busy, but he has time for long walks and talks with me, too. And the children are very happy, and I've published a book. I'm running the Holistic Health Center too."

For the first time in two years I was able to instantly accept an invitation. I was comfortable in my mind about Josh working in Virginia and Paul and Jonathan spending a few days together at home.

"I'll come," I said. "When is it?"

"March 23rd through 29th."

We met in a Pizza Hut on Route 29 in Charlottesville. In spite of no make-up and graying hair, Phyllis was beautiful. Her dark brown eyes smiled at me; her fresh skin glowed with health. We ate, chatted about the pamphlets and preparation tapes that had been sent ahead to us and drove thirty minutes south of Charlottesville to the Institute. We were immediately shown our rooms. Mine had a desk, closet, window, and a bed called a CHEC unit. Like the Captain's bed I had slept on in Holland, the CHEC unit was set in a wooden wall enclosing it on three sides and was curtained on the fourth. Within it, there was a board with panels of lights, headphones, a tape deck, buttons, knobs, and a microphone. It all seemed rather much, but I was so tired that I got into the bed anyway and took a nap.

In response to a dinner bell, I pulled myself together, left my room, and met Phyllis and some others on the way downstairs. We turned out to be a group of two leaders and nineteen participants, most of us professional people: a college professor, a mathematician, an engineer, a mortgage broker, an artist, a doctor, upper-management business people, Phyllis, and me. More men than women, too. Unusual, I thought as we went into dinner.

After we'd eaten, the leaders gave us a little spiel about the technology used in the Institute. Sound based, they said. Called the Frequency Following Response. Nonverbal audio patterns which lead the brain into states associated with deep relaxation and expanded awareness. (I was jotting down notes.) Produces brain waves identical in both brain hemispheres, thus allowing the hemispheres to be focused on the same state of awareness at the same time. Known as Hemispheric Synchronization, or Hemi-Sync for short.

"States of awareness can be changed by the Hemi-Sync signal," the trainer was saying.

"What's that?" the mortgage broker asked.

"Sound pulses in each ear. You won't hear them really. You will experience them. The pulsing will be picked up by your brain."

"Won't we hear anything?"

"You'll hear instructions and the sound of surf."

"Will we have an out-of-body experience?" the mathematician asked.

"Bob Monroe has written two books describing out-of-body experiences but, if that's all you're here for, you're likely to be disappointed. We're going to teach you a process that you can use in everyday life. This week of technique and practice will allow you to tap into your own higher stages of consciousness — even in the middle of a business meeting. By the way, please turn in your watches, time is of no importance here."

Our trainers, Dave and Sherry, continued for another half-hour preparing and affirming us in what we were going to be doing during the coming week, so, although I went to bed a bit anxious, by the next morning, I had a sense of security and safety.

Secretly, I hoped to go out-of-body. Each person, they had told us, was responsible for his or her own experience, which was dependent on the individual's state of being. I determined that I was going to Be My Very Best, but, as I should have remembered, that kind of trying got in my way.

On the audio system in my CHEC unit, Bob Monroe's pleasant voice was saying, "Make yourself comfortable. Relax your mind and your body. Now, pack your concerns into your energy conversion box." I remembered that Dave had said that an energy conversion box was an imaginary storage place for anxieties, fears, expectations, the past, the future, and the family—anything, in fact, that could interfere. Stretched out on my bed, I imagined a metal foot locker with a heavy lid, in which I packed all of the above, and, quite pleased with myself, got ready to begin my first exercise.

"Relax your eyes, your ears, your neck, your scalp," Bob said. I tried to listen and make my mind blank. Instead, my mind put out the garbage, let out the dogs and cats, and reclaimed my watch which had slithered out from underneath the closed lid of the imaginary box. Every time I put it back, it flattened itself and slipped out again. Evidently, to my mind, pancake time was better than no time at all. I found that my excess baggage would not stay in the box either and often would not get into it at all. Sometimes I couldn't even identify it until it became very heavy to carry around. Finally, I worked out a mail slot in the side of my box through which I could slip baggage as soon as I became aware of it. I reassured it that, when the exercise was over, I would release it again.

It took repeated practice before I was able to move easily into the first level of super-consciousness, but, with Bob Monroe's gentle encouragement and the help of the Hemi-Sync, I became able to close my box without my watch slipping out, grab hold of my good electricity, and sink into Focus 10.

"Body asleep, mind awake." I saw a magnificent elephant's head, decorated with a leather headband jeweled with diamonds, rubies, and sapphires, and with blue and scarlet ribboned runners, a head which was so enormous that I could only see as far as its neck. When the session was over and I went downstairs to share my experiences with the others, I described my elephant head, started to say that I wanted to see the whole animal, but said instead, "I guess I'm not ready for the whole picture yet."

"At least you saw a picture," said the stock broker. "I'm afraid I went to sleep."

"I wasn't getting anywhere at all," said the doctor, "so I took off my headset, left the CHEC unit, and came down to get a Coke."

As a group we were beginning to bond together. Often we met in a line outside of the bathroom. (Those long CHEC periods—three of them a day—required an empty bladder.) Besides Phyllis, I was becoming very fond of our trainer, Dave, whose kindness shone out of his brown eyes and whose gentleness was predominant in his unobtrusive voice. I also rather liked the engineer. He took time to try to explain to me the technology in our CHECs. He was much more aware of our surroundings than anyone else and looked around at everything with a measuring eye.

"I've been blocked by a brick wall every time I've tried to move into complete relaxation," he told me one day in the bathroom line. "It's a very well built, carefully mortared wall, and behind that is another wall, and behind that still another one. I've been standing, staring and figuring a way to get by them. If I run around, or climb, or chisel a hole, or knock a wall down with a wrecking ball, there's still the one behind it. Today, I looked them straight in their bricks and said, 'I'm not going to fight you guys anymore!' With that the whole bunch of them disappeared."

"You were fighting a brick wall," I said and went back to my CHEC unit for the next session. In those sessions, we were being taken to deeper and deeper or higher and higher levels of consciousness, and I was finding it easier and easier to change my state of awareness. My CHEC Focus 10 Unit was beginning to seem like my own living room in which I could flick on one or another waking dream.

That day, I found myself on top of a cliff over a deep

abyss. All around me was thick, dark mist. Huddled beside me was a group of students, dressed like monks in simple long, dark gowns. Monks, or perhaps Hassids. I felt that they were there on that cliff in order to practice "trust" and the trust involved jumping off the cliff to sail in the mist. There was a murmuring of questions within their huddle, from which none of them seemed able to break away.

I slipped into and shared the body of one of the monk/Hassids, and together we jumped off the cliff sailing the air currents, dipping into the abyss, wafting gently upwards again. The mist around us was soft and cool, and we flew marvelously. Soon everyone had jumped off the cliff and was gliding about in the misty air.

"Return to Level 1," I heard Bob Monroe's voice saying. I left my monk/Hassid and returned to full physical waking consciousness, realizing that in contrast to my fall from the ledge, this time I had sailed safely.

I thought of that experience as I went down to lunch. Didn't it signify a progression? Certainly I was one of those on the cliff who had practiced trust.

I looked for Phyllis and sat beside her at the long table where we all ate together.

"Let's take a walk on our break after lunch, shall we?"

It was so warm that we needed no coats. Spring had snatched up Virginia. The forsythia was beginning to burst, grass was greening, and the cows in the meadows were calving. There were two brown and white babies standing next to their brown and white mothers. Guernseys, maybe. They rolled their big sweet eyes and mooed at us. We gave them a wide berth as we crossed their pasture.

"How do you feel about the Institute by now, Pecki?" Phyllis asked as we scrambled over the fence between the field and our destination, the lake.

"If you want to know, you should feel my electricity." I held out my hand to her.

"It's surging, isn't it?"

"Yup. I can hardly wait to see what happens during the

rest of the week. I like the group a lot too, particularly because there are men here who are open to new ideas."

"It's because Gateway has a scientific basis. That's why they're open to it."

"You're right. How wise you are, Phyllis." I felt free and happy and delighted with her, so delighted that I put my arm around her and we did a whirling dance down the grassy slope to the lake.

"Stop, Pecki. It's getting slippery."

At that point we skidded and sat down. Having brushed leaves, twigs, and what mud we could off ourselves, we took a walk halfway around the lake. Not too far in the background, there were low rolling blue mountains, with higher, bluer mountains behind them.

"The lake has been stocked, I hear," Phyllis said.

We looked for fish but only saw a few minnows in the shallows.

"Tadpoles," I pointed them out.

"Lu-uvly evening," sang Phyllis after making frog noises in her throat.

"So you had that record too. Tubby the Tuba."

It was only 3:00 when we got back for the next session. I got into my CHEC, put on my earphones, made myself comfortable, knees bent for energy flow, and turned on the Hemi-Sync. I was in Focus 10 when my chest exploded and a purple mountain began to grow out of me. Its wide base was solidly rooted in my heart cavity, and its center kept pushing upwards. Every time I thought it could not possibly grow anymore, it erupted to a new height. I watched it with awe and pleasure. There was no pain and no fear. After I returned to Level 1, I remembered the black-shrouded dripping heart I had held in my hand when Paul and I were driving home from The Program. That black heart had turned into a mighty purple mountain, something strong and glorious, a growth that felt highly positive. I was beginning to communicate with myself in symbols.

But on Wednesday nothing at all happened, no symbols,

no experiences, either spiritual or creative. During the group sharing session, I sat silent and envious listening to the fantastic stories of the others.

"There's this one tiger I ride all the time," said the artist rocking her body and smiling with delight.

"A tiger!" I was more than ever jealous.

"I ride some kind of a large cat too. It's rather sexual," said the mathematician.

"Speaking of sexual, I find that I am getting an erection when the Hemi-Sync starts," said the Cambridge professor. "I try to redirect the energy, not focus on it."

"Does that work?"

"At first, I had a bit of trouble, but now it does."

"Aphrodite isn't only goddess of love, she's also goddess of creativity," said the artist.

So on Thursday morning, I went into my CHEC unit, determined to plug into that sexual energy. I began by picturing the various men in the group while Bob led us from Focus 10 to Focus 15. No response. Some of them were married, some of them didn't appeal to me and others were too young. Then I thought, why not Paul? Zap! He appeared. Zap! My electricity moved into high voltage. I saw above me our two astral bodies — some years younger than they actually were. We were floating through beautiful music, like the music I'd heard in my dream, Pan's music, played on the Jerusalem artichoke. My physical body was asleep on the bed, head on a pillow, arms at my side, spine flattened, knees bent, Hemi-Sync coming through the earphones on my head, but my astral body was making love with Paul, both of us willingly, with great knowledge of each other. I had a front row view of what was going on about two feet above my physical self. Our astral bodies seemed to be covered in a flesh-colored silk casing and were made up of dot-like particles which got darker when touched. Mouths, breasts, legs, we floated entwined, Dante's Paolo and Francesca. Energy waves swirled above, below and through me. I got hotter and hotter. The pleasure was incredible. We laughed together, enjoyed each other, Paul moved towards me and his body merged into mine. We rolled into and out of each other, through each other, two clouds penetrating and separating. Our astral selves watched what was happening and penetrated each other again in a burst of music and ecstasy.

Bob Monroe was talking us down. I zoomed from 15 to 1 and bolted out of my bed.

I wasn't ready to share the experience with anyone but Phyllis. "I just made love to Paul," I whispered to her. "Too bad he wasn't around."

On Thursday afternoon, I had another experience. I saw Anna Frank. It was not my imagination doing it. That was blank. Whatever happened in the CHEC unit seemed to flow in from somewhere in the Universe. I saw her face in a great funnel of energy. She dove straight into my abdomen, unbolted a lock and went back up through the energy vortex. Something in me opened with a jolt. I heard Bob Monroe's voice say, "Release the emotion, bring back the memory." The unlocking I felt released me from my childhood fears. All that sadness was gone, and only love remained.

In an earlier session, I had developed a technique to help me free myself from my physical body. I packed myself in a satin-lined porcelain egg and placed the egg in the metal box amongst other packed-away distractions. As soon as I did this, my astral shape would appear. Sometimes there would be a tussle, but, with the help of some exercises I learned, my astral shape was able to triumph. It could roll out, drift through my bed, and out of my body. This was accompanied by energy rushes as if I were plugged into an outlet where the voltage was being increased.

On Friday, I entered Focus 21. My physical body unbolted at the chest and I whooshed through clouds towards white heat and golden light. I felt music. The heat was terrible but I was determined to go through it. At that, the clouds burst open, the air cooled, and two people walked towards me with open welcoming arms. They were Bubba and Grandmother Zorn. Grandmother Zorn led me by the hand to a glowing woman in a gown of stars. Around us were heat-particles turned into diamonds. From a distance, I heard Bob Monroe's voice calling me back.

In the sharing session, I wrapped a blanket around myself. I was shaking with waves of heat and cold. Was it the refiner's fire? Had my good electricity taken me through it to find my true strength? My good electricity and the love of Grandmother Zorn? Whatever, I wanted to sing and dance for joy.

When it was time to go home, the members of the group signed their names in the dust on my car. I felt that I was driving off with their blessings upon me. I was in a hurry to get home. I could have stopped to see Josh, but I did not. Instead, I winged him my love and drove straight to Sporting Hill Farm, to Paul and Sixer and Dubie and the cats, to the crocus that would be embroidering the path to my front door.

When I turned from Route 95 onto Route 1 at Chadds Ford, I remembered that it was at this spot that I had found in my hand my heart, black-shrouded and dripping. I remembered that that painful, wounded broken thing was now a mountain. Reb Nahman had said, "There is nothing as whole as a broken heart." For five years, my heart had been broken. Now it was whole and filled with joy.